AQA Psychology
A Level Paper Three
Issues and Debates

The Extending Knowledge and Skills series is a fresh approach to A Level Psychology, designed for the greater demands of the new AQA specification and assessment, and especially written to stretch and challenge students aiming for higher grades.

Dealing with the compulsory topic of AQA's **Paper 3: Issues and Debates**, this book is deliberately laid out with the assessment objectives in mind, from **AO1: Knowledge and understanding** material, followed by **AO2: Application** material, to **AO3: Evaluation and analysis** material. Providing the most in-depth, accessible coverage available of individual topics in Paper 3, the text is packed full of pedagogical features, including:

- **Question time** features to ensure that the reader is consistently challenged throughout the book.
- **New research** sections clearly distinguished within each chapter to ensure readers have access to cutting-edge material.
- A clear focus on the **assessment objectives** for the Paper topic to ensure readers know when and where to apply knowledge.
- The use of **example answers with examiner-style comments** to provide greater insight into how to/how not to answer exam questions.

An engaging, relevant and challenging text that broadens student understanding beyond that of the average textbook, this is the essential companion for any student taking the AQA A level Paper 3 in Psychology.

Phil Gorman is an experienced psychology teacher and Assistant Principal Examiner for Paper 3 of the AQA A Level Psychology specification. He has been teaching this subject at A Level for over 25 years and examining for roughly the same amount of time. His examining experience has, in the past, taken him to the position of Chief Examiner for Edexcel A Level Psychology.

Extending Knowledge and Skills series

The *Extending Knowledge and Skills series* is a fresh approach to A Level psychology, designed for greater demands of the new AQA specification and assessment, and especially written to stretch and challenge students aiming for higher grades.

Going beyond the reach of traditional revision textbooks, each book in the series provides wider explanations and greater levels of detail on each of the main topics within each paper option and shows how to apply this knowledge in an exam setting to produce higher tier responses.

Books in the Series:

AQA Psychology A Level Paper Three: Issues and Debates
Phil Gorman

AQA Psychology A Level Paper Three: Relationships
Phil Gorman

AQA Psychology A Level Paper Three: Schizophrenia
Phil Gorman

AQA Psychology A Level Paper Three

Issues and Debates

Phil Gorman

First published 2020
by Routledge
2 Park Square, Milton Park, Abingdon, Oxon OX14 4RN

and by Routledge
52 Vanderbilt Avenue, New York, NY 10017

Routledge is an imprint of the Taylor & Francis Group, an informa business

© 2020 Phil Gorman

The right of Phil Gorman to be identified as author of this work has been asserted by him in accordance with sections 77 and 78 of the Copyright, Designs and Patents Act 1988.

All rights reserved. No part of this book may be reprinted or reproduced or utilised in any form or by any electronic, mechanical, or other means, now known or hereafter invented, including photocopying and recording, or in any information storage or retrieval system, without permission in writing from the publishers.

Trademark notice: Product or corporate names may be trademarks or registered trademarks, and are used only for identification and explanation without intent to infringe.

British Library Cataloguing-in-Publication Data
A catalogue record for this book is available from the British Library

Library of Congress Cataloging-in-Publication Data
A catalog record has been requested for this book

ISBN: 978-0-367-37542-3 (hbk)
ISBN: 978-0-367-37543-0 (pbk)
ISBN: 978-0-429-35500-4 (ebk)

Typeset in Goudy Old Style
by Servis Filmsetting Ltd, Stockport, Cheshire

For all the students who inspired me to produce this book.
Thank you so much for your comments and encouragement.

Contents

1: Introduction 1

2: Gender bias 8

3: Cultural bias 24

4: Free will and determinism 42

5: The nature–nurture debate 60

6: Holism and reductionism 80

7: Idiographic and nomothetic approaches 97

8: Ethical implications of research studies and theory 112

Index 129

Illustrations

Figures

2.1 Ellis's ABC model 12

2.2 Petri dish 17

3.1 Strange situation episodes 29

3.2 Van Ijzendoorn and Kroonenberg's meta-analysis 30

4.1 Maslow's hierarchy of needs 46

5.1 Synaptic transmission 64

5.2 Pavlov's dog 67

6.1 Levels of explanation 82

6.2 Brain image from the Human Connectome Project 85

7.1 Freud's psychosexual stages 101

Tables

3.1 A cross-cultural comparison of obedience rates 28

4.1 Schedules of reinforcement 48

7.1 Research into the encoding specificity principle 100

Chapter 1
Introduction

The aims of this book

This book is intended for A Level Psychology students studying the AQA syllabus and has been developed in order to provide further elaboration for the main Paper 3 topics. This particular book will deal with the compulsory topic of Paper 3, Issues and Debates.

The book has been deliberately laid out with the assessment objectives in mind, so you will find AO1: Knowledge and understanding material first, followed by AO2: Application material, and then AO3: Evaluation and Analysis material.

Each of the assessment objectives will have an injunction/command word or some other indication that will give you an idea of the particular objective being assessed and how you are supposed to answer the question.

AO1 will include some of the following injunctions/commands words that will indicate you are required to show knowledge and understanding:

Compare – Identify similarities and differences.
Identify – Name or state what it is.
Name – Identify using a technical term.
Describe – Provide an account of.
Distinguish – Explain how two things differ.
Explain – Show what the purpose or reason for something is.
Give – Provide an answer from memory or from the information shown.
Outline – Provide the main characteristics.
State – Clearly set out.
What is meant by – Provide a definition.

AO2 will open with some kind of stem which might be in the form of some information which you will need to refer to in your answer. For example:

Question 1

In 2014, 19.7% of people in the UK aged 16 and over showed symptoms of anxiety or depression. This percentage was higher among females (22.5%) than males (16.8%).(mentalhealth.org.uk)

With reference to the information above, what do these statistics tell us about the prevalence of depression by gender?

Alternatively, AO2 questions will provide a description of a scenario with the names of some fictional characters who are involved in a situation that is relevant to an area of psychology. You could then be asked to explain this situation using knowledge derived from the relevant topic. For example:

Question 2

Syd and Ali are discussing the fact that both of them are terribly afraid of dogs. Syd puts it down to a bad experience he had when he was a child after a dog bit him. Ali can't remember having had any bad experiences and thinks that maybe he was just born that way because his dad has the same problem.

With reference to the section above, identify the influence of nature on our behaviour and the influence of nurture on our behaviour.

Questions with a stem like this, which then ask you to refer to the stem in some way, are looking to assess AO2 and you have to make sure that you make clear reference to the stem by using some of the information as part of your answer. You will see examples of these in the coming chapters with some sample answers to show you how to deal with them.

AO3 will include one or both of the following injunctions/commands words, indicating that you are required to demonstrate skills of analysis and evaluation:

Discuss – Present strengths and weaknesses of a topic (in 16 mark questions, this can also require some element of description and can be taken as similar to describe and evaluate).

Evaluate – Make a judgement about a topic with reference to evidence.

One of the important features of this book, and other books in the series to follow, is that there is a clear emphasis on the kinds of skills required for the A Level Psychology exam, so the plenary sections use questions that are focused on exam skills and, at the end of every chapter, there are some exam -style questions with advice on how to answer them and examples of the kinds of answers that could be given to gain very high marks. Key words will be presented in bold and placed in a glossary at the end of each chapter, to make it easier to follow what these words mean and be able to use them more readily yourself.

Further features include an emphasis on new research that is both up to date and challenging, so there will be topics that don't just follow the usual pattern but will make you think again about the kinds of issues and debates that you are studying.

The book also uses the technique of interleaving by bringing back topics from earlier studies to reinforce and consolidate earlier learning. All too often topics that have been studied earlier can be forgotten, and it has been shown that by regularly revisiting these topics, it is possible to remember much more easily than by simply trying to cram them all in at the end. This also fits in well with the synoptic nature of this paper, as you are expected to bring material from other areas of the course into your answers in the issues and debates section of paper three.

What are issues and debates?

Psychology is a subject that is full of questions and controversies, ranging from the seemingly simple question of why we do the things we do to complex controversies such as whether our mind and brain are the same thing. It is worth noting that I said that the first question was *seemingly* simple because although we might say it is fundamental to our understanding of psychology and human behaviour, it is far from simple, as you will see as we go through this book.

As well as continually throwing up such controversies, psychology is a subject that may appear to be based around common sense but is in fact questioning common sense much of the time. In fact, much of the content of this book does just that and takes a large part of the content that is taken for granted concerning human behaviour and turns it on its head.

Interleave me now

Psychology vs common sense

Consider the list of behaviours below. What would common sense say about them? What would psychologists say?

Behaviour	Common-sense view	Psychologist view
In all situations people will follow their own consciences in deciding how to behave		
Eyewitnesses to crimes have very accurate recall about what the offender looked like		
Children can only have one special emotional bond and that's with their mother		
Mental illness is only experienced by a very small number of the population		
Evolution can only explain physical changes, not behavioural changes		
Showing that violent TV is linked to aggression can show us why people are violent in real life		
When we're asleep, our brains are almost completely inactive, like being unconscious		

Hopefully, this comparison shows the clear difference between the ideas we take for granted (common sense) and the ideas we get from psychological research.

Most of the issues presented in this book are there because those studying human behaviour have, at times, not given enough consideration to the effects that they can have, not only on psychological research, but also on our better understanding of human behaviour. Without sufficient consideration of these issues, we can never claim to have provided a full understanding of human behaviour in all of its complexities.

What are issues?

The issues concern some of the problems with research that may be hidden from view unless we make an effort to uncover them and use them as part of a critique of the research that is attempting to explain all human behaviour.

Activity 1: Issues in psychological research

Look at the short list of issues presented below and identify what problems might arise from a lack of consideration of these issues when conducting psychological research. When doing this, try to also identify examples of research where these issues might apply. (*Remember*: ethical issues are not simply the same as ethical guidelines.)

- ethical issues
- gender bias
- culture bias.

You probably came up with some of the points below:

Ethical issues Participants in research might suffer psychological or physical harm, e.g. Zimbardo's Stanford prison experiment
Gender bias The research may not be generalisable to both sexes, e.g. Asch only used men in his research
Culture bias The research may not be applicable to other people in different parts of the world, e.g. Milgram only conducted his research in America

The issues above are the three that will be considered in detail in this section of the course and the above is only a small selection of the points that could be made regarding these three issues. This is particularly true of ethical issues, as the AQA specification identifies the ethical implications of research as the main point, which goes far wider than just the participants in the research?

Question time

What do you think the term 'ethical implications' refers to in the context of psychological research?

One way to think about this question is by looking at the possible effect that psychological research has on individuals or groups within society. If it is seen to have a negative effect, you might want to consider whether the research should have been done in the first place.

An important example of research in this context came from the work of psychiatrist Frieda Fromm-Reichmann in 1948 who suggested that schizophrenia could be caused by both maternal rejection and maternal overprotection, which were behaviours exhibited by the so-called 'schizophrenogenic mother'.

Question time

What do you think the ethical implications of this research might be for the mothers of people suffering with schizophrenia?

Thankfully such ideas have since been rejected and it is now regarded as something of an embarrassment in psychology to have ever believed that such a proposition could be true. However, this embarrassment itself may also have created some negative implications.

New research

The ghost of the schizophrenogenic mother

Josephine Johnston LLB, MBHL

Published in *AMA Journal of Ethics,* September 2013

Johnston suggests that the idea of the schizophrenogenic mother and the subsequent rejection of it following a number of studies and research may have caused a further negative implication.

She suggests that modern psychiatrists have been so haunted by the fear of suffering similar embarrassment that they have become afraid to consider the role of social situations and the family (and the mother in particular) as part of the onset of schizophrenia.

According to Johnston, this is partly shown by the increasing reliance on drug treatments alone in the treatment of children with severe mental disorders. She cites research suggesting that between 1998 and 2007, the number of people being given drug treatment alone rose by 13 per cent. Among children, the situation was even worse with less than half of children aged 2–5 years taking antipsychotic medication, being provided with psychotherapy in a whole year of taking medication!

Question time

What ethical implications are being raised in Johnston's article?

This kind of critical examination of both old and new ideas can help provide a more thorough discussion and greater insights into the causes of human behaviour.

Issues and debates at A Level Psychology are extremely important in the analysis of the material that we are using as part of our attempt to provide a thorough and effective discussion. While it is true that the normal process of evaluation can provide some effective material, a consideration of issues and debates can provide a more thorough understanding.

The debates

The debates are concerned with the basic starting point for all psychological research and the rationale for human behaviour that lies behind such research, e.g. nature vs nurture.

Activity 2: Debates in psychology

Match up the following lists of words to form a pair that show what each debate is called. One of them is done for you to give you an idea of what to do.

Nature   Nomothetic
Free will   Reductionism
Idiographic   Nurture
Holism   Determinism

These are the four debates that you will need to be familiar with for the AQA specification. And each of them has something to say about the both the approach to research that might be taken and, probably more importantly (in most cases), what is the driving force behind human behaviour. You may have noticed that we have already given some consideration to one of the debates in the discussion on the schizophrenogenic mother research above.

> ### Question time
>
> If we argue that schizophrenia has nothing to do with parental treatment and instead is caused by biochemical factors that require drug treatment. Which debate are we looking at?

One of the oldest debates of the four identified above is one that considers the extent to which it is biological or environmental factors that influence our behaviour and this debate goes back thousands of years and across many cultures around the world. Early philosophers such as Galen were theorising about the effect of bodily fluids on our moods and behaviour, while others such as Locke were suggesting that we were all born a blank slate waiting for experience to write on it and shape the course of our lives.

This debate may well be the oldest of those you will study, but it is also the one that most people (including non-psychologists) will have an opinion on and some people will argue is impossible to prove one way or the other. It is of course, the nature–nurture debate. Even though these words only came into use in the sixteenth century, as suggested above they have been hotly debated in one form or another for thousands of years.

> ### Question time
>
> Consider all the things that you are able to do. Are they the result of innate abilities that you were born with or are they developed through experience and learning? Try to consider a behaviour that is just one or the other and then try to convince someone of that argument.
>
> Is it easy to do or do you find that there are as many arguments against your view as there are in support of it.

One scientist believes that he has found the answer and it lies in the new science of epigenetics.

New research

The end of nature vs nurture

Evan Nesterak

Published online, www.thepsychreport.com, 10 July 2015

In the article, Nesterak reports on the work of David S. Moore and his book, *The Developing Genome: An Introduction to Behavioural Epigenetics* (Oxford University Press, 2015).

Moore argues that it isn't important what genes you have, but more what your genes are doing. He goes on to argue that what your genes are doing is influenced by your environment and experiences. Factors such as our levels of stress or nutritional factors can all contribute to which genes are turned on or off and consequently, there is a constant interaction between genes and environment, which makes the debate about either/or meaningless.

Nonetheless, the debate about nature vs nurture continues and undoubtedly will do so as long as there is behaviour that causes some controversy and as long as people are looking for ways to change it.

Summary

This introduction should have got you ready for more of this kind of debate and will hopefully aid you in your further understanding of these fascinating topics.

Chapter 2
Gender bias

Spec check

Gender and culture in psychology – universality and bias. Gender bias including androcentrism and alpha bias and beta bias.

AO1 (Knowledge and understanding): Gender issues in psychology. Does gender play a role in psychological research?

Psychology has, historically, been dominated by men. In attempting to construct a timeline of psychology with my students recently, I found myself falling into this same gender trap. Our first version (guided by me) featured only men. Almost without thinking, I accepted the view that the major branches had all been developed by men and that it was perfectly reasonable to have no women on this timeline (the second version included a number of women).

Such gender bias has been pervasive in scientific research for centuries and this has included psychological research, and maybe still does. This bias towards the focus on male researchers is, though, just one part of the issue of gender bias and, whilst this in itself may cause problems for the representation of women in psychological research, there is a bigger problem that lies beneath the assumptions made by psychological researchers.

Whilst it is a problem if all of the people conducting psychological research are men, it is an even bigger problem if this leads to the conclusion that it doesn't matter as men and women are all the same and therefore we can generalise from the study of men to the rest of the population regardless of gender.

Universality and bias

This brings us to the question of whether it's possible to assume that research carried out on humans can be generalised, regardless of the perceived differences between us. Indeed, in the past and to some extent still today, it has been assumed that we could generalise from the study of animals to human beings and therefore it should be possible to generalise from men to women. Unfortunately, such assumptions have led to some fairly devastating consequences in the field of medical research (thalidomide, DES (diethylstilbestrol), etc.)

The question of the universality of psychological research is one that plagues the subject in most areas. **Universality** would suggest that it is possible to apply the findings of psychological research to everyone regardless of their apparent differences.

This can clearly be seen as a problem when it's only based on a relatively small number of individuals.

The issue of bias is one that continues to raise questions for psychological researchers. **Bias** arises in psychological research when one group or individual is treated differently, and often more favourably, than another.

One particular problem in the process of psychological research is, whether it is possible to free yourself of your own biases and conduct completely value-free research. However good our intentions might be, can we really rid ourselves of these biases? This is a real problem if we look at the possible influence of implicit biases, which are 'discriminatory biases based on implicit attitudes or implicit stereotypes' (Greenwald and Krieger, 2006). According to Greenwald and Krieger, these biases may influence people to operate in a discriminatory manner in spite of the avowed principles of the individuals involved. Consequently, any attempt to be value free and reject the notion of bias may be impossible as it is happening at a level that we are not necessarily aware of.

> ## Question time
>
> What do you think? Is it possible for psychological researchers to be value free or do we just have to accept that all research will be biased, which is OK as long as we know it and accept it? All research can then be judged in the light of these prejudices, without the pretence of value freedom.

Forms of gender bias

Androcentrism

Androcentrism is the tendency to focus attention on males at the expense of females. Andro refers to males and centrism refers to the tendency to 'centre' or focus your attention on something. Psychology has, historically, been accused of this in the research process and the formation of theories. This can lead to either alpha or beta bias.

Alpha bias

Alpha bias is bias that tends to overplay the importance of gender in our understanding of human behaviour and suggests that men and women are completely different. It either implicitly or, sometimes, explicitly suggests that the behaviour of the two should be explained quite differently.

In this case, gender differences are exaggerated as it is assumed that males and females are completely different. In theory, it could work in favour of either males or females as one could be regarded as superior to the other; in reality, however, it is often based on the notion that males are in some way superior to females.

Examples include Freud's work into psychosexual development, which focused on the differences in development between males and females. For example, the notion of penis envy sees women as inferior to men, and Freud even went so far as to argue that femininity is a form of failed masculinity!

Beta bias

Beta bias tends to downplay the importance of gender in our understanding of human behaviour and tends to suggest (as above) that we can ignore the issue of gender as men and women are basically the same – and, therefore, we can just study men, if we wish and apply the results to women.

In this case gender differences are ignored as it is assumed that they have no effect and that men and women are exactly the same!

Examples of research that demonstrate beta bias include the work of Kohlberg and his research into moral development in which he exclusively studied men, although he didn't, in the end, come to the conclusion that men and women were the same but suggested that women were in fact morally inferior.

I think we can see a pattern developing here and, in fairness to both Freud and Kohlberg, they are by no means alone in making these kinds of assumptions. Indeed, many others have both historically and currently fallen into the same trap and could be accused of similar gender bias.

Mini plenary

Match the terms below with the correct definition by writing the appropriate letter next to each term in the box next to each definition:

A – Universality
B – Bias
C – Androcentrism
D – Alpha bias
E – Beta bias

☐ Ignoring or minimising the differences between men and women.

☐ Exaggerating the differences between men and women such that one or the other is devalued.

☐ The tendency to treat one group/individual differently to another.

☐ Applying research to people, regardless of their apparent differences.

☐ Focusing all your attention on males.

AO2 (Application of knowledge): How does the issue apply in practice?

Gender bias and the psychodynamic approach

As previously mentioned, the work of Freud has frequently been regarded as gender biased and often, with good reason, he was accused of ignoring or at least misrepresenting female development as it may not have easily fitted with his overall theory. Of course, Freud is not the only one who was working in a psychodynamic tradition and it may be useful to consider the work of another psychodynamic psychologist to further our understanding of gender bias.

Interleave me now

Bowlby's attachment theory was developed from a psychodynamic tradition, based around the view that attachment is driven by unconscious urges and instinctual biological drives. There are a number of strands to this theory, but it may be useful to focus on one for now.

According to Bowlby (1969), attachment is driven by evolutionary forces linked to survival and, therefore, a baby will attach to someone in order to increase its chances of survival. Such behaviour will involve the drive to find food, but survival is more than just about food and the infant will also seek comfort and security from their attachment figure.

An important aspect of the theory is **monotropy**, which is the view that babies will form one main attachment with someone that is special and different from all other attachments that they may form throughout their lives. Who is going to be this **primary attachment figure**? Their mother of course! For Bowlby, the source of this was both a biological bond built up in the womb and an urge to attach or imprint upon the first thing they see after birth, which is likely to be their mother.

Inevitably, this has led to both support and criticism for Bowlby in arguing that he is, on the one hand, recognising the importance of bonding for the newborn and the difficulties that arise without such a bond (supporting him), but, on the other hand, that he is devaluing the role of the father and exaggerating the differences between men and women in the attachment process.

Much of the supporting research for this is based on the study of **neonates** and the immediate reaction of infants to their potential attachment figures, which understandably has meant studying the behaviour of them with their mothers. This means that it may be difficult to separate off the study of attachment from the baby's interactions with and reactions to their mother, until such a time when men start to give birth that is!

Question time

What type of bias may Bowlby be accused of in putting forward his attachment theory?

Why do you think he ignores the role of the father?

Is there evidence to suggest that attachment is not monotropic?

What are the implications of this theory for adopted babies?

Gender bias and psychopathology

Psychopathology is concerned with the symptoms, explanation and treatment of mental disorders and has attracted a lot of interest in terms of the gender division for such disorders. One area that has particularly come into focus is depression and the main focus of explanation for depression within the A Level syllabus has been on the cognitive approach.

> ## Interleave me now
>
> **Cognitive explanations for depression** have focused on the role of internal mental processes in understanding why someone becomes depressed, as the suggestion is that it is not the event itself that causes a person to become depressed but their reaction to it. This means that external factors such as traumatic experiences in themselves are not the cause of the disorder but the internal response to these events. One example of this is the cognitive vulnerability-stress model of mental disorders, which suggests that some people are more vulnerable to the effects of stressful events due to their negative thinking style.
>
> As explained by Ellis (1957), negative thinking can lead someone to react inappropriately to stressful stimuli and put that person well on the road to depression.

Ellis's ABC model

Ellis believed that everyone's thoughts are rational at times and irrational at other times. Good mental health is the result of rational thinking – thinking in ways that allow people to be happy and free of pain. Psychological problems occur if people engage in irrational/faulty thinking to the point where it becomes **maladaptive** for them, so they are not happy and free from pain.

Ellis's model was developed to explain the response to negative events, i.e. how people react differently to stress and adversity.

The model (see Figure 2.1) provides the sequence of the process: A – the adversity or event to which there is a reaction; B – the belief or explanation about why the situation occurred; C – the consequence – the feelings and behaviour the belief now causes.

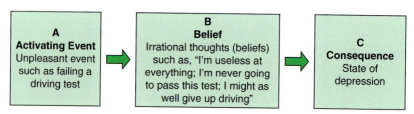

Figure 2.1 Ellis's ABC model

Mental health statistics – depression

In 2014 19.7 per cent of people in the UK aged 16 and over showed symptoms of anxiety or depression. This percentage was higher among females (22.5 per cent) than males (16.8 per cent). (mentalhealth.org.uk).

> **Think!**
>
> What do these statistics tell us about the prevalence of depression by gender?
>
> What does that mean for the cognitive vulnerability-stress theory of depression?

The statistics are clearly showing that women are diagnosed with depression more frequently than men and, if we are to believe the cognitive explanation, this would suggest that women are more prone to negative thinking than men and that it is this rather than some other factor that explains their likelihood of becoming depressed.

Question time

How might Ellis explain these statistics?

Is there another explanation for them?

Could the cognitive assumptions made about these statistics be regarded as an example of alpha bias, beta bias or androcentrism?

Mini plenary

Can you think of other examples of research that demonstrate the following?

Alpha bias
Beta bias
Androcentrism

Place some examples in the table below. Ensure you provide examples that include androcentrism, alpha bias and beta bias as well as none of the above.

Androcentrism	Alpha bias	Beta bias	No bias at all

AO2 (APPLICATION OF KNOWLEDGE)

AO3 (Analysis and evaluation of knowledge): Is it really an issue?

Is science sexist?

Science has traditionally been regarded as work that is carried out by men, who are able to study phenomena objectively and rationally. Such traits have stereotypically been applied to men and less often to women.

This has meant that scientific research has come to be regarded as sexist due to its characterisation of women as either temperamentally inferior or intellectually inferior – or possibly both. Darwin himself argued that women were at a lower stage of evolution than men, which has been used to provide support for this distinction.

John Horgan (2017) argued that science was sexist and still is, first because women in science are harassed and discriminated against by men and second because male scientists regard them as intellectually inferior. Explanations for this have been given a scientific basis, historically by Darwin and more recent explanations have suggested that women are less ambitious, prone to neuroticism and have more of an interest in people than things.

It seems as though alpha bias has become institutionalised (see **institutional bias**) in science and this might help to explain how and why sexism has become so much a part of scientific and psychological research.

In response to Horgan's claims, Claire Lehmann and Debra W. Soh (2018) argued that science should not be considered sexist as those who argue such things are missing the point that studies have shown that women are more neurotic and are less ambitious!

This seems to demonstrate that little progress is made in challenging sexism in science and that it may take a little longer for gender bias to be eradicated from scientific research.

What are the implications of alpha bias?

If the differences between men and women are exaggerated, by suggesting for example that women express more negative emotions than men and use more negative emotion-related coping strategies than men, then a result of this could be to believe that women are less able to cope with negative situations and therefore not suited to certain jobs.

For example, Schmitt et al. (2008) found that women scored more highly on neuroticism (also supported by many other studies) and because of this many have suggested that neuroticism is more of a female trait. Inevitably, this isn't a positive finding and those that have looked into it seem to suggest that it should be explained by evolutionary considerations rather than social ones.

Unfortunately, this type of research tends to ignore the social context in which it takes place and therefore it may not be able to provide a full picture of the reasons for this finding. It may be that culture, **socialisation**, prejudice and discrimination have more to do with the creation of more negative emotions than any of these studies are prepared to give credit to.

It's a shame they didn't think of that themselves really!

What are the implications of beta bias?

If the differences between men and women are ignored by most researchers, when the majority of participants in, for example, the medical sciences are men, then the results could be very damaging for women.

This could almost be as damaging as the research that was only conducted on animals being applied to human beings. The result of that was that drugs were developed and given to pregnant women that resulted in both birth defects and serious, life-threatening illnesses developing in their offspring.

Nielsen et al. (2017) reported: 'Of the ten drugs withdrawn from the US market between 1997 and 2000, eight involved health risks for women that may have been avoided if more attention had been devoted to gender-related and sex-related factors.'

According to their study, one of the major factors in deciding whether gender issues were taken into account was the sex of the lead researcher/author, which brings us back to the old chestnut of the position of women in academic research, particularly in health-related research.

The conclusion of the study is that none of this will change until more women are being placed in positions where they are the lead researcher/author and that will require a massive change in the culture of academic research.

Is it possible to conduct **feminist** research?

The question here is whether it is possible to conduct research that is not gender biased and therefore non-sexist.

In the 1980s and 1990s, there were attempts made to consider the question of what kind of psychological research could be produced that was non-sexist and possibly even feminist.

At a convention of the American Psychological Association in 1980, Dee Graham and Edna Rawlings argued that not only should good feminist research use mostly women, but that it should also adopt qualitative methods such as interviews and personal documents.

On the one hand, this is questionable on the basis that it is potentially replacing one form of gender bias with another (it could also be accused of alpha bias) but it may actually be too simplistic to deal with what is a very complex problem.

Peplau and Conrad (1989) argue that simply replacing male participants with females or replacing experiments with interviews will not serve to remove bias and sexism in the research process and may, in fact, help to hide it as important research into stereotyping and discrimination carried out by men (as well as women) may not get done.

These attempts to conduct feminist research may just serve to reinforce stereotypes as they are seen by men as female issues and not (as they need to be) as mainstream and worthy of study by all psychologists, regardless of gender.

Can we legislate away sexism?

Much of what has been presented here is quite depressing and it seems as though the prospect of change is fairly unlikely. But surely all we need to do to address this is change the law and things will get better for women. After all, the law on voting was changed by campaigning women who forced the government to change the law and bring about equal rights, at least in terms of voting.

However, this point fails to address the fact that there have been many changes in the law designed to end **sexual discrimination**, and yet such discrimination is clearly still happening today.

In the UK, the Equal Pay Act, the Sex Discrimination Act and the Equal Opportunities Commission all came into effect in 1975 and yet women are still on average paid less than 90 per cent of men. In a report for the British Council (2016), Janet Veitch argued that while it is important to have legislative change, unfortunately, it's not in itself enough to bring about change at the speed that is required. Not until social norms are changed in relation to stereotypes and role models will we see a significant improvement in the treatment of women.

On the face of it, this should be fairly simple but, in reality, it has proved extremely hard to change what are deeply ingrained prejudices among both men and women, even in the so-called developed world, and it will require more than a female prime minister to bring about real change.

Think!

In what ways does psychology itself help to perpetuate gender stereotypes? What could be done to change this?

Mini plenary

In the table below, identify an evaluation point in the section on the left. Tick the appropriate box to show whether the point relates to alpha bias, beta bias, androcentrism, or just gender bias in general. Then, in the section on the right, explain why. (You can tick more than one box.)

Evaluation point	Alpha bias	Beta bias	Androcentrism	General gender bias	Explanation

A modern issue: #metoo

The issue of gender bias in psychological research has been discussed within the wider context of sexism in society as a whole and even though most people would recognise that such sexism is common in society, it has been brought into sharper focus by the #metoo issue that has been raised by women in the entertainment industry. Unfortunately, it is becoming clear that this is also an issue for women involved in scientific research too.

New research

Why science breeds a culture of sexism

David Batty and Nicola Davis, 7 July 2018

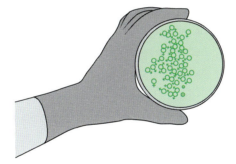

Figure 2.2 Petri dish

One of the problems of sexism within scientific research has been investigated by *The Guardian* in research involving more than 30 victims of sexual harassment in university science departments. The victims, all from the US and UK, told the researchers that there is a male-dominated culture in these departments that makes it more difficult to challenge than in other workplaces. They argue that the expectation of late-night working combined with the isolated nature of the work create the perfect conditions for sexual harassment to thrive.

This situation is bad enough for the individual as it affects their career and mental health, but it may also cause them to leave science altogether, which can create problems for society as talented individuals who could make important discoveries may be lost. According to the article, this behaviour has led to what some are calling science's 'Weinstein moment', as a number of well-known scientists from prestigious universities have been accused of **sexual misconduct**.

Unfortunately, it seems that even when women do speak out, they are either not believed or have pressure applied to them to withdraw their complaint – and it is not just men who are doing this. It is as though the positions that those accused hold and their reputations are so important that institutions will go to any lengths to protect them. There appears to be something of a 'great man' culture among those around the accused who are trying their best to defend them because of their great scientific achievements. However, the authors of the article argue that the focus should not be on the 'poor man', as he has been the focus of attention for 2,000 years, but on the 30, 100 or 1,000 victims (we cannot know how many there really are) who have not gone on to make their own fantastic achievements just because they were the victims of the behaviour of a man!

Question time

How does this article relate to the issue of gender bias?

What do you think is meant by the phrase 'science's Weinstein moment'?

What might be the implications, if the above article is accurate?

What is the way forward? Is there anything that can be done to change this? Will it be easy?

Chapter plenary

1. What is meant by the term bias?
2. What is meant by the term universality?
3. What is meant by the term gender bias?
4. What is meant by the term alpha bias?
5. What is the meant by the term beta bias?
6. What is meant by the term androcentrism?
7. Which areas of psychology have been shown to contain some form of gender bias?
8. What research is there to support/oppose this view?
9. What other examples of research in psychology are there that are relevant to this issue?
10. What evidence is there to suggest that science is sexist?
11. What evidence is there to show the implications of alpha bias?
12. What evidence is there to show the implications of beta bias?
13. What are the arguments for and against feminist research?
14. What evidence is there to show that sexism can't be legislated away?
15. Can you provide modern examples of gender bias in psychology or science?

Glossary

Key word	Definition
Alpha bias	The tendency to overplay the importance of gender in our understanding of human behaviour and suggests that men and women are completely different. It either implicitly or, sometimes, explicitly suggests that the behaviour of the two should be explained quite differently.
Androcentrism	The tendency to focus attention on males at the expense of females.
Beta bias	The tendency to downplay the importance of gender in our understanding of human behaviour and suggests that men and women are the same and that the behaviour of the two should be explained identically.
Bias	One group or individual is treated differently and often more favourably than another.
DES	The abbreviated form of the drug, diethylstilbestrol, used to prevent miscarriages in pregnant women. It had also been tested on animals but had serious side effects for human babies, including malformation of reproductive organs, infertility and even cancer.
Feminist	Refers to someone who is trying to achieve equality for women.
Gender bias	A preference or prejudice towards men or women, such that one is treated more favourably than the other.
Institutional bias	Bias that is built into the normal procedures and practices of an institution and is not just down to the behaviour of one individual.
Maladaptive	Not adjusting adequately to the environment or situation.
Monotropy	The belief that infants form one attachment that is special and different to any other.
Neonates	Another word for newborn babies.
Primary attachment figure	The person who is the most important attachment figure in an infant's life.
Sexual discrimination	Any action that causes a more favourable outcome for one sex at the expense of another.
Sexual misconduct	Any unwanted behaviour of a sexual nature that is directed towards someone against their consent.
Socialisation	Features of the external world that my affect our behaviour as we grow and develop, including other people, social situations and experiences.

AO3 (ANALYSIS AND EVALUATION OF KNOWLEDGE)

Key word	Definition
Thalidomide	The name of a drug used to treat morning sickness in pregnant women, which was sold as an over-the-counter drug. It had been tested on animals with no side effects but when used with humans led to limb deformities in the newborns.
Universality	The possibility of applying the findings of psychological research to everyone regardless of their apparent differences.

Plenary: Exam-style questions and answers with advisory comments

Question 1.

Outline what is meant by bias in psychological research. [2 marks]

Marks for this question: AO1 = 2

Advice: In a question like this, it's important to make sure you are outlining what is meant by bias in general, rather than gender bias. However, it must be placed in the context of psychological research, so it would be useful to provide a relevant example. There is no need to provide any analysis or evaluation as both of the marks are for AO1: Knowledge and understanding.

Possible answer: Bias involves one group or individual being treated differently to another, often one group is treated more or less favourably than another. An example from Freud's research is that he regarded femininity as a form of failed masculinity.

Question 2.

Researchers have identified a new area of the brain that is important in problem solving and rational thinking. They studied 500 men and found that this area was particularly active when given logical thinking tasks to carry out. They believe that there is no evidence of similar activity in the brains of women.

With reference to the section above, explain what is meant by androcentrism. [2 marks]

Marks for this question: AO2 = 2

Advice: In this question, it's really important to recognise that both marks are for AO2, which means that you have to show the skill of application to the stem. You will still need to show an understanding of androcentrism, but this time by picking out the references to it from the information you have been given. There is still no need to analyse or evaluate.

Possible answer: The article is heavily male-focused because they are suggesting that men have an active area of the brain that women don't have. This is androcentric as it is comparing women against men and suggesting that women don't have problem-solving and rational thinking skills, even though they only studied 500 men and there is no mention of studying women.

Question 3.

Discuss gender bias in psychological research. Refer to at least two topics you have studied in your answer. [16 marks]

Marks for this question: AO1 = 6 and AO3 = 10

Advice: This question is looking for both the skills of knowledge and understanding and those of analysis and evaluation. As there are 6 marks for AO1 and 10 for AO3, there should be greater emphasis on the evaluation. However, all such extended writing questions are marked holistically and therefore it is important that the knowledge is accurate and detailed and that the evaluation is clear and effective.

Possible answer: Psychological research is most commonly associated with men. When we talk about psychology, we might talk about Milgram or Zimbardo or maybe even Sigmund Freud. Rarely do we talk about Ainsworth or Klein or indeed Anna Freud. The fact that the most famous psychologists are men is unlikely to be an accident, in fact it is more likely to result from some form of bias.

Bias is either a deliberate or accidental feature of some work and tends to favour one thing/group over another. In relation to gender there are a number of forms of bias that have been identified.

Alpha bias occurs when the differences between men and women are overplayed such that men and women are regarded as completely different in all areas of life. This might sometimes involve women being regarded as better than men at some things, e.g. childcare. But it's more likely to involve the idea that men are better than women at things and will often not just focus on things that require greater height or muscle mass but will often refer to things that are 'technical' and not regarded as part of a woman's domain, such as driving! A psychological example of this can be seen from the area of mental disorders where women are believed to be more prone to depression due to their higher levels of emotionality, which might make them more prone to mood swings. Whereas men are regarded as more rational and therefore less likely to suffer.

Unfortunately, these views have become so prevalent that Horgan has argued that science has come to regard women as intellectually inferior and used this as an excuse to discriminate against women. Horgan has used the example of ideas being taken from Darwin and those that claim that male and female brains are entirely different to justify the idea that women are more neurotic and more interested in people than things. This claim has been argued against by Lehmann and Soh (2018) who suggest that Horgan is missing the point as studies have shown that women are more neurotic, which, from their point of view, justifies the treatment of women and might help explain why women are more likely to be diagnosed with depression.

The implications of this type of thinking can create serious problems and can cause negative reactions towards women in many areas of life. For example, Schmitt et al. (2008) found that women scored more highly on neuroticism and, because of this, many have suggested that neuroticism is more of a female trait. This will make it hard for women to be considered for jobs that require the ability to cope under serious pressure, even though this research fails to acknowledge contextual factors in any of these studies and as such fails to provide the full picture and only serves to endorse popular and often ill-founded stereotypes.

Beta bias on the other hand occurs when the differences between men and women are ignored or downplayed such that men and women are regarded as essentially the same. This will usually be used as an excuse to not need to study equal amounts of men and women as 'there's no need' if everyone is basically the same. Beta bias suggests that as results from studies of men can just as easily be used to apply to women as there is no real difference and therefore studies solely of men are perfectly fine.

The dangers of beta bias are more than just the issue of emotional harm brought about by prejudice, they can cause serious health problems too.

Nielsen et al. (2017) reported that, of the ten drugs withdrawn from the US market between 1997 and 2000, eight involved health risks for women that may have been avoided if more attention had been devoted to gender-related and sex-related factors.

This shows that the danger of ignoring the differences between men and women is a serious risk to the health of everyone.

Androcentrism is an extension of beta bias as it takes the whole notion of ignoring the differences between men and women to a new level. This involves almost completely excluding women from the whole debate, in favour of men.

The answer to this may be to try to go the opposite way and push for a feminist approach to research, involving one that takes a more 'gynocentric' approach, which involves focusing on women at the expense of men.

At a convention of the American Psychological Association in 1980, Dee Graham and Edna Rawlings argued that not only should good feminist research use mostly women, but that it should also adopt qualitative methods such as interviews and personal documents. This was being pushed as it was believed that women would be better served by non-experimental methods.

However, this approach may just be replacing one problem with another, as important research that could come from men would be excluded and we would possibly just be replacing one type of bias with another.

The issue of women's rights and the push for equality has been heightened in recent times by the #metoo campaign, which began with celebrities and has now spread to other areas of life. This came mostly from the inability of the government and legal system to deal effectively with sexism. In spite of having laws spanning back fifty years, we still have massive divisions between men and women in terms of pay and top jobs. It seems unlikely that waiting for someone else to do it for you is a strategy that women can put much faith in.

References

Batty, D. and Davis, N. (2018) Why science breeds a culture of sexism. *The Guardian*, 11 July 2018.

Bowlby, J. (1969) *Attachment and Loss*. New York: Basic Books.

Ellis, A. (1957) Rational psychotherapy and individual psychology. *Journal of Individual Psychology*, 13: 38–44.

Graham, D.L.R. and Rawlings, E.I. (1980, September) Feminist research methodology: Comparisons, guidelines and ethics. Paper presented at the annual meeting of the American Psychological Association, Montreal, Canada.

Greenwald, A.G. and Krieger, L.H. (2006) Implicit bias: Scientific foundations. *California Law Review*, 94 (4): 945–968.

Horgan, J. (2017) Darwin was sexist, and so are many modern scientists. *Scientific American*, 18 December 2017.

Lehmann, C. and Soh, D.W. (2018) A different take on sexism in science. *Scientific American*, 11 January 2018.

Nielsen, M.W., Andersen, J.P., Schiebinger, L. and Schneider, J.W. (2017) One and a half million medical papers reveal a link between author gender and attention to gender and sex analysis. *Nature Human Behaviour*, 1 (11), Letters. www.nature.com/articles/s41562-017-0235-x (accessed 26 June 2019).

Peplau, L.A. and Conrad, E. (1989) Beyond nonsexist research: The perils of feminist methods in psychology. *Psychology of Women Quarterly*, 13: 379–400.

Schmitt, D., Realo, A., Voracek, M. and Allik, J. (2008) Why can't a man be more like a woman? Sex differences in big five personality traits across 55 cultures. *Journal of Personality and Social Psychology*, 94 (1): 168–182.

Veitch, J. (2016) Can we legislate away sexism? Report to the British Council, 3 March 2016.

Chapter 3
Cultural bias

> **Spec check**
>
> Gender and culture in psychology – universality and bias. Cultural bias including ethnocentrism and cultural relativism.

AO1 (Knowledge and understanding): Cultural issues in psychology. Does culture play a role in psychological research?

As a teacher of psychology, it has always been clear that psychological research has been dominated by Western, and in particular US, researchers. An analysis of one textbook by Smith and Bond (1998) found that 66 per cent of the studies were American, 32 per cent were European and 2 per cent were from the rest of the world. On one occasion when I was teaching, I spoke to my students about a study conducted in China and, after noting how unusual it was, I decided to question my students on why it might be that we look at so few Chinese studies in psychology. One student suggested that it might be because there are a lot fewer Chinese people in the world than there are American because China is a lot smaller than the USA! Rather quickly, this turned into a geography lesson as I didn't feel I could let this person continue through life with that belief. However, this does raise an interesting issue, because if the issue were based purely on numbers of potential studies per head of population, then most studies should be conducted on Chinese people. In fact, most studies are conducted on Americans and specifically American students, which suggests that psychologists are not taking much notice of cultural differences and are working on the basis that psychological concepts are universal and not affected by cultural factors.

Universality and bias

This brings us back to the question posed in the previous chapter of whether it's possible to assume that research carried out on humans can be generalised, regardless of the perceived differences between us. If this assumption is correct, then all well and good and we can carry on our merry way, safe in the knowledge that we are doing the right thing. If we are wrong, however, then we have a problem and we need to start taking cultural differences a lot more seriously, as we are basing our whole discipline around research that only applies to a small fraction of the world's population.

As discussed in the previous chapter, the question of the universality of psychological research is one that plagues the subject in most areas. **Universality** would suggest that it is possible to apply the findings of psychological research to everyone regardless of their apparent differences. In relation to culture, this could be seen as an even bigger problem than gender bias as it is applying findings based on a comparatively smaller percentage of individuals.

The issue of bias is one that continues to raise questions for psychological researchers. **Bias** arises in psychological research when one group or individual is treated differently and often more favourably than another. In the context of **culture**, the main issue is that the differences between people are being ignored and therefore the bias here is at the level of assuming that the culture of other nations is so insignificant, or at least so insignificantly different, to be not worthy of study. Or maybe, it's just easier to study those around you and therefore the issue is one of laziness!

> **Think!**
>
> What are the reasons for this apparent bias? Is it based on the notion of universality? Is it just laziness? Or are there other reasons why there are so few people from other cultures being studied as part of psychological research?

Ethnocentrism

Ethnocentrism is the tendency to focus attention on your own culture or ethnic group at the expense of other cultures and ethnic groups. Ethno refers to an ethnic group and centrism refers to the tendency to 'centre' or focus your attention on something. Psychology has, historically, been accused of this in the research process and the formation of theories. This could be regarded as simply an error or oversight on the part of researchers or it could be seen as being based on a belief that some cultures or ethnic groups are superior to others and therefore the others should be judged by the standards of the superior group. This is infinitely more serious, as while it may be forgivable to be ignorant about differences, it isn't if you are deliberately excluding certain cultures or ethnic groups.

Cultural relativism

Culture refers to the norms and values of a particular group that have been established over time through the process of socialisation. **Cultural relativism** involves accepting that these norms and values are different and that it's not possible to create a universal set of laws or rules that apply to everyone regardless of culture and that doing so would fall into the trap of ethnocentrism. However, it is very difficult to understand these norms and values if you have not grown up within that culture or spent a considerable amount of time within it. Any attempt to study another culture without having this understanding may still create problems as you could still be using your own norms and values to make sense of behaviour that can only be understood by those from that culture.

One way of looking at this is from the points of view of etic and emic approaches to understanding cultural differences. These terms were first used by Kenneth L. Pike and applied to linguistics in that an etic approach would use phonetics, which are overall structures of sound within all languages, and an emic approach would use phonemics, which are sounds that are specific to a particular language and can only be understood by a native speaker of that language. Looked at in this way, it is easy to see where mistakes can be made as it may be possible to learn another language but still find it difficult to make yourself understood to people within the country using that language.

An etic approach suggests that it is possible to take a general approach to studying other cultures, using universal concepts or theories that can be applied cross-culturally regardless of their differences. The idea of **imposed etic** suggests that standards of behaviour from one culture are being applied to people from another culture. This usually takes the form of applying a standard of behaviour that has been created in one part of the world, e.g. Ainsworth's research into attachment in America, and applying it to people from another part of the world, e.g. attachment types in Japan.

An **emic approach** is much more open and suggests that it is only possible to understand the behaviour of other cultures from within that culture, using ideas and concepts that have been taken from that particular culture rather than some other one. In this sense, research would need to do more than simply study people from other cultures but would need to have a deeper understanding of the culture that is being studied and be able to see things from that culture's point of view.

Think!

How could research be conducted using an emic approach? Who would need to do the research? What method could be used to collect the data?

True cultural relativism would have to accept that behaviour can only be understood in relation to the culture in which it is being studied and therefore can only be applied to the culture from which it is drawn. Unfortunately for US and UK researchers, this doesn't just mean that we have to treat cross-cultural research with this caution, it means we have to use the same caution in all research. Therefore, any research conducted in the US or UK can only be applied to those specific cultures and not universally across the globe – which might be difficult for many to accept!

Mini plenary

Without referring back to the text, provide definitions of the following terms:

Universality
Bias
Ethnocentrism
Cultural relativism
Imposed etic

AO2 (Application of knowledge): How does the issue apply in practice?

Cultural bias and social influence

Social influence is concerned with the influence of social situations on behaviour and as such expected forms of behaviour or norms are particularly important. This is one area where cultural bias may become a little more obvious and one area where the need for cultural relativism may be extremely important. The study of obedience has been the subject of much criticism for its ethical flaws, but it is also worth considering the potential cultural bias and how obedience research may give further insight into this issue.

Interleave me now

Milgram's obedience to authority study was intending to consider the issue of whether or not 'Germans are different'. Milgram (1963) wanted to find out if there was something about the German personality that had made them become so hostile to other ethnic groups that they committed the atrocities of the holocaust. Adorno had previously suggested that an authoritarian personality might explain such prejudice and, therefore, it may be that the German personality was explained by the sorts of factors that Adorno had identified as leading to such a personality, e.g. harsh parenting.

Of course, we know that Milgram never got round to studying Germans as he believed that he had identified a different cause of such attitudes, which was situational forces and an agentic shift. This meant that anyone regardless of ethnicity or culture could engage in such behaviour given the right (or perhaps wrong!) situational factors. Therefore, it's not due to culture nor indeed personality but to the pressure of the situation. Effectively, this means that there was a '**perfect storm**' of factors that came together in Germany at that time to create the circumstances that led to the holocaust.

There is at least anecdotal support for this proposition from a range of other countries and situations that have experienced broadly similar events, from Armenia to Cambodia, Rwanda, Bosnia and, more recently, Darfur. These reasonably diverse examples give support to the view that it may be situational factors that are responsible for such atrocities and this notion can therefore be applied to each of the specific circumstances.

On the face of it, this is useful for a culturally relative view as we are not then imposing a view taken from the study of one group, e.g. Americans, on to anyone else. Milgram suggested it was nothing to do with general ideas about personality but was actually to do with specific situations. However, this idea has been both supported and challenged by various replications of an experiment that everyone seemed to agree should not be done again! Table 3.1 gives some information on the cross-cultural replications of the Milgram study.

Table 3.1 A cross-cultural comparison of obedience rates in replications of Milgram's standard conditions (adapted from Blass, 2012)

Author	Country	Rate of obedience (%)
Ancona and Pareyson (1968)	Italy	85
Edwards et al. (1969)	South Africa	87.5
Mantell (1971)	Germany	85
Kilham and Mann (1974)	Australia	28
Shanab and Yahya (1977)	Jordan	73
Miranda et al. (1981)	Spain	50
Gupta (1983)	India	42.5
Schurz (1985)	Austria	80

Blass (2012) suggests that these studies show a remarkable level of similarity to the results of the Milgram study, so we may be able to assume that as they are conducted in different countries then there is considerable cross-cultural support for Milgram.

However, it has been suggested by Bierbrauer (2014) that we need to look at these results more closely and consider a number of important points:

1. Most of the studies were actually conducted in the West and may be culturally similar to the US.
2. We have to be careful about assuming that the meaning of obedience is the same in each of these countries, particularly those that were non-Western, e.g. Jordan and India.
3. How can we be sure that the status of scientists (highly regarded in the West) is the same in all other cultures?

Question time

What type of bias may Milgram be accused of in putting forward his idea that the obedience **paradigm** explains all obedience to authority?

Why do you think he didn't go on to study Germans?

Is there enough evidence to suggest that the paradigm can be applied cross-culturally?

What are the implications of this paradigm for our understanding of obedience worldwide?

Cultural bias and attachment

One of the classic studies of **attachment** type was done by Mary Ainsworth. The 'strange situation' studies allowed us to recognise types of attachment in infants from their responses to a series of artificially created scenarios involving the infant, their mother and a stranger. From this study Ainsworth was able to identify three types of attachment that are present in different infants depending on the behaviour of their mother. These three types have been investigated cross-culturally and the findings have created both support and opposition to Ainsworth's ideas.

Interleave me now

The study of attachment types was conducted by Ainsworth and Bell (1970) using the strange situation paradigm, which involved the series of episodes and observations shown in Figure 3.1.

Episode	Events	Attachment Behavior Observed
1	Researcher introduces parent and baby to playroom and then leaves.	
2	Parent is seated while baby plays with toys.	Parent as a secure base
3	Stranger enters, is seated, and talks to parent.	Reaction to unfamiliar adult
4	Parent leaves room. Stranger reponds to baby and offers comfort if baby is upset.	Separation anxiety
5	Parent returns, greets baby, and offers comfort if necessary. Stranger leaves room.	Reaction to reunion
6	Parent leaves room.	Separation anxiety
7	Stranger enters room and offers comfort.	Ability to be soothed by stranger
8	Parent returns, greets baby, offers comfort if necessay, and tries to reinterest baby in toys.	Reaction to reunion

Note: Episode 1 lasts about 30 seconds; each of the remaining episodes lasts about 3 minutes. Separation episodes are cut short if the baby becomes very upset. Reunion episodes are extended if the baby needs more time to calm down and return to play.

Figure 3.1 Strange situation episodes

Ainsworth used the list of observations on the right of Figure 3.1 to establish the attachment type of the child and concluded that the ability to use the parent as a secure base while exploring, a moderate level of separation anxiety, a healthy level of suspicion towards the stranger and the ability to be comforted upon the mother's return were all indications of a secure attachment. Any other reactions could be placed into one of two types that either showed a low level of trust (resistant types) or a low level of interest (avoidant types) in the mother and were classified as insecure. She further concluded that these types were an indication of the mother's level of responsiveness to their child. Sensitive mothers who respond quickly and appropriately to their infant's needs (the majority) produced securely attached children (70 per cent of the sample studied) but mothers who were unresponsive or inconsistently responsive produced insecurely attached children. Unresponsive mothers produced avoidant types and inconsistently responsive mothers produced resistant types.

Further studies in other cultures culminated in a meta-analysis of a number of them by Van Ijzendoorn and Kroonenburg in which they were able to produce statistics to show the percentage attachment types for 32 studies using the strange situation paradigm across eight different countries. Figure 3.2 shows their findings.

Country	Number of studies	Percentage of each attachment type		
		Secure	Insecure-avoidant	Insecure-resistant
Great Britain	1	75	22	3
Germany	3	57	35	8
Netherlands	4	67	26	7
Sweden	1	74	22	4
Japan	2	68	5	27
Israel	2	64	7	29
United States	18	65	21	14
China	1	50	25	25
Mean		**65**	**21**	**14**

Van Ljzendoorn & Kroonenburg (1988) meta-analysis of studies comparing attachment type across different cultures

Figure 3.2 Van Ijzendoorn and Kroonenberg meta-analysis

Van Ijzendoorn and Kroonenberg set out to test whether the attachment types were universal and would be the same or similar from one place to another or were culturally specific and would provide a variety of different results.

Think!

What do these figures tell us about the universality of attachment types?

Which countries were different?

What does this tell us about those countries?

Do the figures suggest that some countries are better than others, if so which?

Is this a valid conclusion?

Van Ijzendoorn and Kroonenberg were able to argue from this that there is a high degree of similarity between countries, and that those that had different levels might be best understood in terms of differences in parenting style.

Question time

Is there a problem in the conclusions drawn about the other countries in this study? Do the conclusions have any negative implications?

Are there any other conclusions that could be drawn about this study?

What type of bias may Van Ijzendoorn and Kroonenberg be guilty of in their conclusions?

How else could these results be interpreted?

Mini plenary

Can you think of other examples of research that demonstrate the following?

Ethnocentrism
Cultural relativism

Place some examples in the table below.

Ethnocentrism	Cultural relativism

AO2 (APPLICATION OF KNOWLEDGE)

AO3 (Analysis and evaluation of knowledge): Is it really an issue?

Do Western methods work in other cultures?

One of the problems faced by psychological research is the extent to which the methods chosen are appropriate for studying people in other cultures.

Mary Ainsworth's work has been recognised as ground-breaking and the strange situation paradigm has been regarded as one that contains a high degree of validity in the study of attachment types. However, it is questionable whether this approach is suited to other cultures, which may give different meanings to identical behaviours.

Buil et al. (2012) have suggested that the **construct equivalence** of behaviours must be considered as to whether or not a behaviour means the same thing in one culture compared to another, e.g. observing a child crying hysterically at being separated from its mother may be interpreted as signs of a resistant attachment type to some, but as extremely secure to others. Similarly, seeing a child play happily with a stranger may be a sign of avoidance to some but a sign of independence to others.

Parenting style is not an easy thing to judge within the same culture, never mind between different cultures, and, as such, it may be a very difficult construct to measure from the point of view of just one culture or indeed hemisphere.

Are there more differences between cultures or within cultures?

Culture is not just a concept that applies to different countries, as there are many cultural differences within the confines of one country, something that is likely to be particularly true of very large countries with a large, widely dispersed population. It may be that the differences within a culture (a so-called subculture) are just as big, if not bigger than the differences between two closely related, but separate, cultures.

Differences *between* cultures are referred to as intercultural differences and can be seen from studies that have compared different countries. Differences *within* cultures are referred to as intracultural differences and can be seen from studies that have compared different groups within the same country. This was identified as a particular issue within the Van Ijzendoorn and Kroonenberg study as they accepted that their findings showed more differences within the same country than between each country, which isn't particularly surprising as they showed few differences between different countries.

However, it should still be noted that the majority of the studies were conducted within the US (18 out of 32), so their meta-analysis is more of a study of the differences between attachment studies in the US than one of any real cross-cultural value anyway.

Is everything culturally relative?

It may be the case that we need to consider the cultural relativity of all human behaviour, particularly as the majority of psychological studies have not only taken place in the US but also with a non-diverse sample of college students. However, it may be the case that there are still some behaviours that can be regarded as universal. As Fox (1973) said: 'We could not plead against inhuman tyrannies if we did not know what is inhuman.'

According to Norenzayan and Heine (2005), there are some psychological phenomena that appear to have universal properties or at least to have been drawn from a wide variety of cultural samples: research into human emotions, sex differences in homicide and sex differences in mating preferences to name but a few. These examples seem to support the notion that there are some forms of human behaviour that could be called universal and are either not culturally relative or have cultural diversities that are consistent enough to support the notion of universality.

For example, the work of David Buss (1989) into sex differences in mating preferences did show some cultural diversity but the diversity was consistent with the level of gender inequality within a society, such that, in the end, the tendency towards cultural difference was highly predictable and could be seen as **functionally universal** as they served a useful function in all of the cultures studied in spite of the differences between them.

This means that it may be possible to identify functionally universal forms of behaviour even when we appear to have found some cultural differences in the exact expression of these behaviours across the world.

Is it possible to take a truly emic approach?

The question here is whether it is possible to take a fully emic approach and work as an insider if you are attempting to study a culture that is not your own.

In her classic research into gender differences within Papua New Guinea, Margaret Mead (1963) attempted to immerse herself in the culture of the group that she was studying. She spent many months living as part of the community and became well known among the many tribes that she encountered. In this sense, Mead's work could be seen as an attempt to avoid imposing an etic onto the groups that she was studying. Indeed, her work was able to identify many differences in gender-related behaviour between the diverse groups that make up the population (believed to be one of the most culturally diverse countries on the planet) and was also able to go against the idea that there may be universal gender roles that are the same the world over. However, in her time there, Mead became known as a benefactor to many (employing people to build her a dwelling) and regarded with suspicion by others, so it remains questionable whether she was able to really study the group as an insider.

An alternative approach to this might be to accept that you are unable to rid yourself of your own values and accept the fact that you may be imposing your own etic on to the group being studied. Indeed, David Buss decided to study a vast range of cultures across the world in his study of mating preferences from the comfort of his New York office. However, Buss did use local researchers to deliver his surveys, so it may be that even though the questionnaire was standardised, the fact that it was being implemented by locals may have meant that their understanding of their own culture allowed them to get a less biased point of view.

The notions of emic and etic are clearly difficult to get over and may in the end prove insoluble, but, as long as there is an acceptance that there may be some form of bias within these studies, then perhaps we can stop attempting to create universal truths from them.

What are the implications of ethnocentrism?

Failure to recognise cultural differences and simply working on the basis that your own understanding is right, not only constitutes a form of ethnocentrism but also creates significant problems for people from other cultures seeking medical help, particularly in the area of mental health.

If clinicians are unaware of the cultural significance of certain forms of behaviour, then the result for those from other cultures can be devastating as all of their behaviour will be viewed from behind a cloak of cultural ignorance and certainty that the clinicians' perceptions are correct.

Gorman and Cross (2011) argue that Anglo-Celtic cultures take a very stiff-upper-lip approach to pain that is not recognised by all cultures. In Anglo-Celtic cultures overt expressions of pain can be regarded as attention-seeking or, worse, as expressions of some form of mental health problem. This can place people from other cultures in difficult situations when dealing with clinicians who are making judgements about their behaviour and mental health.

This could lead to some people being wrongly diagnosed with mental health problems simply due to a lack of understanding of the cultural norms for that group. This can be taken one step further when we take account of the considerably larger number of people of West Indian origin being diagnosed with some form of psychosis.

Think!

In what ways does psychology itself help to perpetuate cultural **stereotypes**? What could be done to change this?

Mini plenary

Using the evaluation points above, try to evaluate the following statement:

It's impossible to avoid cultural bias in psychological research.

Arguments for:

Arguments against:

A modern issue: black lives matter

The issue of cultural bias in psychological research has been discussed without really referring to the possibility that such bias might be based on stereotypical ideas of what certain cultures or ethnic groups are like, i.e. racism. The issue of racism has been brought into sharper focus by the 'Black lives matter' campaign in the US. It has been argued that the shooting of and general attitude of the police towards black people is the result of a form of **racial profiling** that identifies black men as being potential criminals and potentially dangerous.

New research

Racial profiling and implicit bias

Laura Maguire, 18 June 2017

In the article, Maguire considers the practice of racial profiling that involves the police and security services targeting people for investigation because of their race, ethnicity or national origin. The question posed in the article isn't so much whether this practice is wrong, because it obviously is, the question posed is 'why is it wrong?'.

In modern society, profiling has become a commonly understood term as most people have watched TV crime dramas involving police specialists using complex processes to uncover the identity of some unknown offender. According to Maguire, the difference between this and racial profiling lies in the complexity of the profiling. Racial profiling is too simplistic, involving crude stereotypes that are based on generalisations about people simply due to their membership of a particular group.

Maguire goes on to question the claim made by some people in America that the higher proportion of certain ethnic groups in prison is a justification for this form of profiling. She argues that just because there are more people from black and minority ethnic groups in prison for a crime like marijuana possession doesn't mean that they are actually more likely to commit the crime. According to her, white people are more likely to be in possession of marijuana, it's just that black people are more likely to be arrested for it. Why are they more likely to be arrested? Because of racial profiling of course. This makes black people more likely to be stopped and searched, more likely to be pulled over in their cars, even though, statistically speaking, they are less likely to be using marijuana than white people.

Maguire argues that this kind of racial profiling isn't just a problem for individual racists but actually becomes a problem for the whole law enforcement institution. It doesn't actually matter whether a police officer has explicitly racist beliefs or not, the problem comes from the fact that it is a reflection of racist attitudes that stem from and help to reinforce racist institutions. There is a kind of 'implicit bias' that makes a police officer think that a black person driving through a rich, white neighbourhood is 'out of place' and therefore decides to pull the black person over. It could just as easily be a black police officer doing this, because they are operating under the cloud of the same implicit bias. This implicit bias causes people to behave in ways that they would say they oppose because they have internalised the kind of stereotypes that arise from this form of bias.

Question time

How does this article relate to the issue of cultural bias?

Why do you think they refer to this as a form of implicit bias?

Does this implicit bias apply to cross-cultural research in psychology? If so, in what way?

What is the way forward? Is there anything that can be done to change this? Will it be easy?

Chapter plenary

1. What is meant by the term bias?
2. What is meant by the term universality?
3. What is meant by the term ethnocentrism?
4. What is meant by the term cultural relativism?
5. What is the meant by the term imposed etic?
6. What is meant by the term emic?
7. Which areas of psychology have been shown to contain some form of cultural bias?
8. What research is there to support/oppose this view?
9. What other examples of research in psychology are there that are relevant to this issue?
10. Do Western methods work in other cultures?
11. Are there more differences between cultures or within cultures?
12. Is everything culturally relative?
13. Is it possible to take a truly emic approach?
14. What are the implications of ethnocentrism?
15. Does the idea of implicit bias mean that it's impossible to avoid cultural bias in psychological research?

Glossary

Key word	Definition
Attachment	A close meaningful bond, usually between two people, in which both find it hard to be separated.
Bias	One group or individual is treated differently and often more favourably than another.
Construct equivalence	The thing being studied means the same to everyone across different measures/cultural groups (similar to construct validity).
Cultural relativism	The recognition that different cultures have different norms and values and no attempt should be made to apply universal values to them.
Culture	The norms and values of a particular group or of a whole society that have been developed over time, through the process of socialisation.
Emic approach	Recognising the differences between cultures and using values from within that culture to understand them, rather than using values from another culture.
Ethnocentrism	The tendency to focus on a person's own cultural/ethnic group at the expense of another.
Functionally universal	It has the same function across all different cultures.
Imposed etic	The tendency to apply standards from one culture to people from another culture.
Paradigm	A set way of doing or studying something that has become the established approach among most researchers.
Perfect storm	When a number of factors occur at the same time causing an event to be unusually bad or significant.
Racial profiling	A practice believed to be employed by those in authority when deciding who to question/pick out for further investigation. It is based on perceived racial/ethnic backgrounds.
Stereotype	A widely held and fixed belief about someone based on their membership of a particular group/culture.
Universality	The possibility of applying the findings of psychological research to everyone regardless of their apparent differences.

Plenary: Exam-style questions and answers with advisory comments

Question 1.

Explain what is meant by cultural bias in psychological research? [2 marks]

Marks for this question: AO1 = 2

Advice: In a question like this, it's important to make sure you are outlining what is meant by cultural bias, rather than just bias in general. As the question asks about psychological research, it would be a good idea to refer to an example. There is no need to provide any analysis or evaluation as both of the marks are for AO1: Knowledge and understanding.

Possible answer: Cultural bias refers to the tendency to treat one group more favourably than another based on their culture. It may also involve using your own culture as a template. For example, Ainsworth's strange situation might be seen as culturally biased as it was based on a Western view of motherhood.

Question 2.

Judged by Western standards, not making eye contact when you speak to someone is terribly rude. If you travel around the world, you will often come across people who don't make eye contact when you speak to them and you may find it very hard to understand.

With reference to the section above, explain what is meant by ethnocentrism.
[2 marks]

Marks for this question: AO2 = 2

Advice: In this question, it's really important to recognise that both marks are for AO2, which means that you have to show the skill of application to the stem. You will still need to show an understanding of ethnocentrism, but this time by picking out the references to it from the information you have been given. There is still no need to analyse or evaluate.

Possible answer: The article refers to judging something by Western standards, which suggests people are only seeing it from the point of view of their culture. They are not recognising that in some cultures it might not be regarded as rude to avoid eye contact when speaking, in fact, it might be the other way round and not recognising this could be seen as ethnocentric.

Question 3.

Discuss cultural bias in psychological research. Refer to at least two topics you have studied in your answer.
[16 marks]

Marks for this question: AO1 = 6 and AO3 = 10

Advice: This question is looking for both the skills of knowledge and understanding and those of analysis and evaluation. As there are 6 marks for AO1 and 10 for AO3, there should be greater emphasis on the evaluation. However, all such extended writing questions are marked holistically and therefore it is important that the knowledge is accurate and detailed and that the evaluation is clear and effective.

Possible answer: Most of the psychological research published seems to be from Western culture. indeed in one textbook, Smith and Bond found that 66 per cent of the studies referred to were American, 32 per cent European and only 2 per cent from the rest of the world. This seems to suggest that there may be a bias in psychological research towards Western ways of thinking and Western ideas about behaviour.

This dominance of Western research is likely to have an effect on the kind of research that is carried out in other cultures and the conclusions that are drawn from it.

One area of potential bias in psychological research relates to the approach that researchers take to studying other cultures and concerns whether they are prepared to try to understand the norms and values of the other culture or whether they are simply going to use their own. An etic approach involves using your own norms and values to guide your research so that you may have a pre-established idea of what you want to study, perhaps based on work previously carried out, and you use that to study other cultural groups.

An example of this can be seen in the use of the strange situation to study attachment types in other cultures. Ainsworth had used the strange situation procedure to identify different attachment types and from this had made a clear distinction between secure and insecure attachments, the former being the good one. In the USA, this had shown that secure was the dominant type with over 65 per cent being of this type.

Van Ijzendoorn and Kroonenberg created a meta-analysis of studies that had used the same procedure to study attachment types in other cultures and, whilst they did find that the dominant type was secure in all cultures, they also found some differences in the percentages of the types in different cultures, specifically they found significantly more insecure types in Germany, Japan and Israel.

Some attempts have been made to explain these differences with references to parenting style in these other countries, which may or may not be true, but the fundamental problem here is that the studies all used the strange situation procedure, which was developed and used in America and therefore may not represent the way that child rearing is conducted in these other countries.

Buil has suggested that the construct equivalence of these measurements should be considered as it may be that what appears to be a reasonable measure of security in one country may not be so in another. Seeing a child screaming because its mother has left the room may be a sign of insecurity to some but may be seen as a sign of a strong attachment to others. Therefore, it's hard to judge unless you understand the context/culture in which it takes place.

Furthermore, one of the things found in the meta-analysis was that there were actually more significant differences in attachment types within each culture that there was between each culture, suggesting that it may not be possible to come up with a set standard for attachment type as it differs so much by subculture, never mind by culture.

This type of research could be regarded as ethnocentric as it is judging the behaviour of people in other cultures against some agreed standard in the West. This type of judgement can have severe effects for other cultural groups in areas such as health and illness, particularly mental health. According to Gorman and Cross, it's normal for people in Anglo-Celtic cultures to take a stiff-upper-lip approach to pain but not necessarily so in other cultures. Consequently, when people in other cultures have a different reaction, it can be regarded as neurotic or even worse psychotic by clinicians in a country with an Anglo-Celtic culture.

This lack of understanding of the norms of other cultures has had devastating effects in a range of situations and has recently come to the fore with the black lives matter campaign in the US. It seems as though police forces and other officials have been engaging in racial profiling to decide who is and isn't a dangerous criminal, resulting in some people being misjudged and as a result being shot and killed.

The answer to this may be to take more of an emic approach in cross-cultural research and attempt to understand other cultures on their own terms by engulfing yourself in their culture.

This approach was adopted by Margaret Mead in her study of tribes in Papua New Guinea with whom she spent many months immersing herself in the culture, which enabled her to have an insider's view of family life and, in particular, gender roles in the country. She identified a range of different gender roles, some of which were similar to those in the West with others being the opposite, alongside other differences. She believed that this showed that gender roles were culturally relative and were dependent on the needs of the people in the culture and should not be regarded as universal.

However, although Mead had attempted to throw off her Western values, it seems as though this wasn't always recognised by the locals, who may have seen her in some cases as a potential benefactor, and many of them worked for her and may have behaved/explained things in ways that they thought she wanted so the validity of these findings may be in doubt.

This might point towards the idea that it is very difficult to take a truly emic approach as you may always end up imposing your views on the culture being studied or at least on the conclusions you draw. David Buss attempted to study cross-cultural attitudes to relationships by employing locals to conduct his questionnaire in 37 different countries. He managed to find that cultural attitudes to mating preferences across the world were remarkably similar.

This was supported by Norenzayan and Heine who suggest that there are many behaviours that are universal, with sex differences in mating preferences being one of these and, more than that, the slight cultural differences that were found by Buss might still be consistent with the general level of gender inequality in each culture. These small differences may in fact be functionally universal, in that they serve the same purpose in whichever culture they appear, in this case working out the evolutionary demands of mating.

References

Ainsworth, M.D.S. and Bell, S.M. (1970) Attachment, exploration, and separation: Illustrated by the behavior of one-year-olds in a strange situation. *Child Development*, 41: 49–67.

Bierbrauer, G. (2014) Stanley Milgram's legacy to cross-cultural psychology. How would the results of his obedience studies replicate in non-Western cultures? *Journal Psychologie des Alltagshandelns/Psychology of Everyday Activity*, 7 (2).

Blass, T. (2012) A cross-cultural comparison of studies of obedience using the Milgram paradigm: A review. *Social and Personality Psychology Compass*, 6 (2): 196–205

Buil, S., de Chernatony, L. and Martinez, E. (2012) Methodological issues in cross-cultural research: An overview and recommendations. *Journal of Targeting, Measurement and Analysis for Marketing*, 20: 223–234.

Buss, D.M. (1989) Sex differences in human mate preferences: Evolutionary hypotheses tested in 37 cultures. *Behavioral and Brain Sciences*, 12 (1): 1–14.

Fox, R. (1973) *Encounter with Anthropology*. New Brunswick, NJ: Transaction.

Gorman, D. and Cross, W. (2011) Cultural issues in mental health. In: *Mental Health Nursing: Dimensions of Praxis*. Melbourne, Australia: Oxford University Press, pp. 427–442.

Maguire, L. (2017) Racial profiling and implicit bias. *Philosophy Talk*, 18 June 2017. www.philosophytalk.org/blog.racial-profiling-and-implicit-bias (accessed 29 June 2019).

Mead, M. (1963 [1935]). *Sex and Temperament in Three Primitive Societies*. New York: William Morrow.

Milgram, S. (1963). Behavioural study of obedience. *Journal of Abnormal and Social Psychology*, 67: 371–378.

Norenzayan, A. and Heine, S.J. (2005) Psychological universals: What are they and how can we know? *Psychological Bulletin*, 131 (5): 763.

Smith, P.B. and Bond, M.H. (1998) *Social Psychology Across Cultures*, 2nd edn. London: Prentice Hall International (also 1999, Needham Heights, MA: Allyn & Bacon).

Van Ijzendoorn, M. H. and Kroonenberg, P.M. (1988) Cross-cultural patterns of attachment: A meta-analysis of the strange situation. *Child Development*, 59: 147–156.

Chapter 4
Free will and determinism

> **Spec check**
>
> Free will and determinism: hard determinism and soft determinism; biological, environmental and psychic determinism. The scientific emphasis on causal explanations.

AO1 (Knowledge and understanding): The free will and determinism debate. What do we mean by free will and determinism? What is the difference between hard and soft determinism? What do we mean by biological, environmental and psychic determinism?

Free will

Free will is a concept that many people might aspire to or already believe that they have. In many ways, it is what makes us an individual, distinct from others in that we are able to make our own choices and decide which option to take from a number of possibilities. There is a recognition that we do respond to biological drives and environmental pressure, however, it does not see these as truly governing our behaviour. Free will could be regarded as the essence of humanity in that it distinguishes us from animals as we are not simply responding to our instincts or to the demands of the situation in which we find ourselves. Consequently, this is closely related to the humanistic view of behaviour.

Determinism

The belief that behaviour does not happen by choice but is instead governed by forces that are beyond our control. There are two versions of this concept: hard and soft determinism.

Hard determinism

This is the view that we have no free will at all and that all behaviour is driven by uncontrollable forces. It is the view that all behaviour has a cause and as the cause can be put down to something that is (usually) testable then we can predict behaviour in the same way that we can predict the outcome of a science experiment. The forces that guide our behaviour can be biological (such as genes or hormones), environmental (such as work or school) or possibly even psychic (from our unconscious mind).

Soft determinism

This is a compromise position between free will and hard determinism. This view suggests that we have a limited range of choices as most behaviour is decided by some forces but that it is still possible to make choices on a day-to-day basis. This is strongly related to the idea of cognitive mediating factors as seen in Bandura's (1977) theory, which suggests that we can choose from the behavioural options presented to us.

Biological determinism

A view that follows on directly from the assumptions of the biological approach to human behaviour and argues that all behaviour is, in the first instance, driven by biological factors (genes, hormones, the nervous system, etc.) If we attempt to explain any form of human behaviour, we must at some point come back to the view that our responses are triggered by neural signals in our brain leading to messages being sent to our muscles telling us to behave in some way. All of this is ultimately governed by our genetic make-up, and therefore biology can explain all forms of human behaviour. Alongside this, we could argue that all behaviour is adaptive and therefore governed by evolutionary factors.

Environmental determinism

This view follows on from the behaviourist approach and the belief that all behaviour is the result of some form of conditioning. Skinner regarded free will as an 'illusion' and suggested that most, if not all behaviour is driven by its consequences. We have learnt through positive and negative reinforcement that behaviour has consequences and therefore we don't make decisions, we merely follow the path that has been set out for us to follow by parents, teachers, bosses, etc.

Psychic determinism

This view follows on from the psychodynamic approach and the belief that all behaviour is driven by our unconscious mind. Freud saw behaviour resulting from innate instincts that lead us into childhood conflicts. These conflicts are repressed into our unconscious mind and push our behaviour in certain directions, generally to avoid anxiety or to satisfy the demands of different parts of our personality.

The behaviour that results is not under our conscious control but merely the ego's response to anxiety-causing dilemmas.

Question time

What choice do you have about how to behave on a day-to-day basis? Can you decide not to go to school or college, not to go to work? Not to wear any clothes today?

Try to think of examples of behaviour where you have a completely free choice? What would happen if you did make that choice? Would there be any consequences?

Have you ever wondered, 'why do I do that'?

It should be clear that most of our choices are made based on a very limited range of possibilities. Imagine if you told your parents that you aren't going to school or college today. What would they say? What would they do? What would your school or college do if you didn't turn up?

What if everyone decided that they didn't want to go to work anymore? What would happen to the economy and society as a whole? One way or another, we have to do these things otherwise society as we know it would start to fall apart.

The scientific emphasis on **causal explanations**

The biological and behaviourist approaches are both approaches that believe that psychological phenomena can be observed and tested, and that from them we are able to identify the causes of behaviour. The emphasis is on the development of general laws to explain behaviour, for example, within classical conditioning. This focus on **general laws** and observed phenomena leads both approaches towards the use of scientific methods. For both, experimentation involving the testing of hypotheses in controlled environments is very important in identifying the causes of behaviour.

Using this approach, we are able to make human behaviour much more predictable and show that in the same situation, most if not all behaviour will go in the way predicted and this makes it possible to find ways of dealing with that behaviour. To accept that behaviour is decided by individual choice leads to the possibility that every individual will behave differently in a given situation and, ultimately, resulting in chaos!

Think!

Do the biological and behaviourist approaches work in the ways suggested above? Are there general laws for most forms of behaviour? Do we all act like robots, completely controlled by external forces? Where else does our behaviour come from? Can science explain all forms of behaviour?

Mini plenary

Below is a numbered set of terms used in the section above and a lettered set of definitions. See if you can match the correct number with the correct letter.

1 Free will	A All behaviour is driven by biological factors such as genes and the nervous system.
2 Determinism	B The ability to make our own choices and decide what to do from a range of possibilities.
3 Hard determinism	C All behaviour is driven by our unconscious mind.
4 Soft determinism	D We have no free will at all, and *all* behaviour is driven by uncontrollable forces.
5 Biological determinism	E Behaviour does not happen by choice but is driven by forces beyond our control.
6 Environmental determinism	F Recognition that some behaviour is driven by other forces, but we do have some control.
7 Psychic determinism	G Behaviour is the result of some form of conditioning.

AO2 (Application of knowledge): How does the debate apply in practice?

Humanistic psychology and free will

Humanism is the only approach that advocates complete free will. All of the other approaches see our behaviour as being controlled in some way. It assumes that all individuals are unique and therefore not merely a product of their genes or environment. It accepts that there are internal and external influences on behaviour but argues that we are free to regulate our own behaviour as we are not passive recipients of these influences. Instead, we are involved in a process of actively shaping our lives and experiences.

Interleave me now

Maslow's hierarchy of needs

An example of this is shown in the work of Abraham Maslow (1943) and his hierarchy of needs (Figure 4.1).

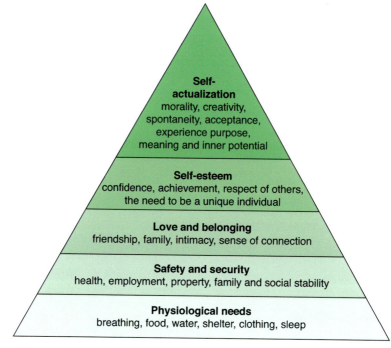

Figure 4.1 Maslow's hierarchy of needs

Maslow accepted that in order to function a person must satisfy basic physiological needs first and if these weren't satisfied then all human behaviour would be motivated around trying to satisfy those needs. However, he regarded these needs as largely temporary and just a means to an end and that the focus of motivation theory should be on the ends rather than the means of achieving them. Higher human goals lie at a different level than basic physiological drives.

Nonetheless, it is true to say that a human being must achieve the more basic needs before moving on to the others. However, as soon as the more basic need is fulfilled, the human will strive to achieve the next need, and so on. This notion of striving is very important to Maslow and it is that which pushes us towards **self-actualisation** – and it's that which separates us from animals. According to Maslow, we do not simply rest when we have satisfied our basic needs, as an animal may do, we move on to the satisfaction of the higher needs and even when we have achieved all of them, we don't rest until we have achieved self-actualisation, 'What a man can be, he must be' (Maslow, 1943).

The main focus of research then, should be that which is experienced by the individual, rather than what forces are acting upon the individual. This approach is quite anti-scientific as it rejects the notion that it's possible to create general laws or rules of behaviour. The focus should be on the quality of experience from the subjective point of view of each individual, looking at the quality of human experience rather than the quantity of it.

Question time

What is self-actualisation? How do we achieve it?

Does Maslow believe in complete free will?

How would this approach go about studying human behaviour?

Is this approach useful for studying all human behaviour?

Behavioural approach and environmental determinism

The behavioural approach has a number of assumptions about human behaviour but one of the most influential is the view that behaviour is governed by conditioning. Skinner famously argued that free will is an illusion and believed that it was possible to control behaviour given the right circumstances. Skinner's view is that all behaviour is learned as result of reinforcement and therefore behaviour can be shaped by controlling the consequences of behaviour. If I say jump, and you jump and get some form of **reinforcement**, then you are more likely to do it again in the future.

Interleave me now

Skinner's work on **schedules of reinforcement**

Skinner (1965 [1953]) believed that all behaviour is the result of reinforcement contingencies, therefore behaviour is nothing more than a set of responses to environmental triggers. In Skinner's 'brave new world', our behaviour would be controlled from birth through the tight control of what we are exposed to. If we are exposed to the right kind of reinforcement, then there is no reason why we should have to put up with bad behaviour as there will be none in our tightly controlled society.

Skinner used a Skinner box (see Table 4.1) to show how reinforcement could be used to make a rat respond by pressing a lever. In the constant reinforcement phase and during training, every time the rat presses the lever, it gets a reward of food. This acts as a **positive reinforcer** to encourage the rat to do it again. The law of effect (actually developed by Thorndike) stated that any behaviour that is followed by pleasant consequences is likely to be repeated, and any behaviour followed by unpleasant consequences is likely to be stopped.

This was how Skinner planned to control behaviour – by controlling the consequences of behaviour. If we can get the schedule of reinforcement right, we can easily control rats' and humans' behaviour.

Table 4.1 Schedules of reinforcement

Schedule of reinforcement	Response rate	Pattern of response	Extinction rate
Fixed ratio (reinforced for every *n*th response)	Very high	Steady with low ratio. Brief pause after each reinforcement with very high ratio	Slow with high ratio
Variable ratio (reinforced after varied no. of responses)	Highest	Constant, no pauses	Very slow
Fixed interval (reinforced after a fixed period of time)	Lowest	Long pause after each reinforcement followed by gradual acceleration	Slow with long intervals
Variable interval (reinforced after a varied period of time)	Moderate	Stable	Slower than fixed interval with same average interval

Table 4.1 shows each of Skinner's schedules of reinforcement and provides a comparison of the response rate for each one as well as showing how regular the pattern of response was for each and how quickly the response became extinct. When using constant reinforcement, Skinner found that the rats would have a very low response rate, long pauses in their responses and their responses became extinct very quickly.

Question time

What does this tell us about which schedule works best? Why does it work best?

Why doesn't constant reinforcement work very well?

What does this tell us about how easy or otherwise it is to control animal behaviour? Does it tell us anything about human behaviour?

What areas of life can this be applied to?

Mini plenary

Can you think of other examples of psychological research that demonstrate the following?

- Free will
- Hard determinism
- Soft determinism
- Biological determinism
- Environmental determinism
- Psychic determinism

Place some examples in the table below.

Term	Examples of psychological research			
Free will				
Hard determinism				
Soft determinism				
Biological determinism				
Environmental determinism				
Psychic determinism				

AO3 (Analysis and evaluation of knowledge): How useful is the debate?

What are the benefits of free will?

If we take Maslow's hierarchy of needs as a starting point and the view that once we have satisfied our basic physiological needs, we can then move on to higher needs and the striving for self-actualisation, then it should be clear that there are major benefits for believing in free will.

Striving to achieve beyond what we can currently do may be the thing that makes us human, that fuelled our evolution from apes through to Homo sapiens (if that's what you believe). While our unconscious mind may be responsible for our baser instincts in a kind of Freudian way, it could be that our conscious mind is where our potential achieving decisions are made. Why do we learn to ride a bike? To play a musical instrument? Or to journey into space?

Klemm (2010) has argued that the 'zombian' idea of human beings as being at the whim of their subconscious leaves no room for personal achievement nor indeed responsibility and, as such, not only makes it difficult for us to strive to achieve anything but also means that no one is responsible for their actions – and therefore there should be no punishment for crime nor any accolade for success. After, all wasn't it inevitable this was going to happen?

A belief in free will allows individuals to take credit for their success and their failure, but also to take responsibility for their actions. How can we tell ourselves that effort is the key to success, if we believe that actually it isn't because we are all merely the product of our genes and environment anyway? How is it possible to change the direction of someone's life if it is already set in stone?

Is free will possible?

The problem with the free will argument is that it believes that all human striving comes from within each individual and that leads to all forms of positive outcomes for the individual and society. The belief that you have this kind of control makes people feel better about themselves and believe that everything is fair and everyone gets what they deserve, when, in fact, it could just be down to trial and error and getting the odd lucky break.

Bargh and Earp (2009) have argued that no matter how positive the benefits of belief in free will are, a positive illusion is still an illusion. Unfortunately, it is too often the case that a belief in free will is selective in that we take credit for our successes but not for our failures – as shown by many experiments into attribution theory. This seems to point to the idea that belief in free will is more about the management of our self-esteem than it is to do with any real motivation for behaviour.

In the way outlined by Skinner, this suggests that the motivation for behaviour comes from the consequences of the behaviour. If the consequences of behaviour are seen to be positive then the behaviour is likely to be engaged in, if not then it will not be engaged in. It could be, then, that all of these advances and technological achievements came about as a result of raising self-esteem or some other form of personal or indeed financial reward.

It seems as though it may be impossible to separate off free will from determinism in much the same way as it's impossible to separate nature from nurture. Any behaviour that appears to be motivated purely by choice could be seen in the context of some form of learning and therefore the only behaviour that is not determined could just be random luck and even that probably has its determinants in some past events.

Is soft determinism a better alternative?

To say that all behaviour is determined seems very pessimistic, but to say that it's all free will seems unrealistic, consequently, soft determinism offers a useful alternative and might be seen as a useful compromise. Soft determinism suggests that we may not have true free will, but we do have some choice over our behaviour. We are able to choose from a limited range of options as our cognition helps us to make sense of the possibilities rather than just react to them. However, **cognitive neuroscience** has enabled us to delve further into the neurological basis of these choices and show that it isn't quite that simple.

The discovery of the **readiness potential** (Libet et al., 1983) has shown that apparently voluntary actions are in fact triggered at an unconscious level before they enter consciousness. This suggests that even what appears to be completely voluntary free action is in fact planned for in the nervous system a split second before becoming conscious, and therefore it is still determined to some extent.

Participants in the Libet study were asked to note the position of a moving dot when they were aware of their conscious decision to move their finger. Using EEG measurements from their scalp, Libet was able to show that, while there was a pre-movement build-up of electrical activity 550 ms before the movement, the participant only became consciously aware 200 ms before the movement. This left a period of 350 ms, which came to be known as the readiness potential, 350 ms before they were consciously aware of their decision.

This shows that even something as random as a decision to move your finger has a neurological basis and is therefore still determined. So, the cognitive approach and, in particular, cognitive neuroscience appear to have provided support for determinism rather than supporting a middle ground.

What are the limitations of scientific study?

The use of experiments has been highly beneficial in developing our understanding of the causes of behaviour as the ability to isolate variables and make precise measurements has strongly advanced through developments in cognitive neuroscience.

However, scientific study can only measure so much. Yes, we can read measurements of an EEG based on timing instruments that go down to the thousandth of a second and beyond, but can we be sure that what we are measuring is really what we think, in short, can we be sure of the validity of these scientific measurements.

Lavazza (2016) has argued that there are many possible interpretations of these results, given the simplified nature of the experiment, and that there have been many excellent experiments that have shown different interpretations of similar phenomena, using more advanced instruments. One such criticism that remains is whether you can be sure that the neural activity you are measuring is the result of the current activity or the result of previous similar encounters, which are recognised by the brain and activated in response to this situation.

Therefore, the use of neuroscience to measure these instances may be highly precise and very carefully controlled but may still not actually be measuring what it is hoping to measure.

Is qualitative research the way forward?

There are many who would argue that a focus on causal explanations can use more than one approach and that a mixed method approach may help in the discovery of the causes of human behaviour. If we really want to understand causality, then maybe we should use more than just numbers as our measurement as words can give us a more complete picture.

The **positivist approach**, made popular by the ideas of Karl Popper and others, has maintained a high level of dominance in psychology, as it was believed that the search for empirical evidence was the only way forward if we were to explain human behaviour. But maybe this is only true if we want to control human behaviour. If we are less concerned with the control of human behaviour then, maybe we can use a more qualitative approach.

The British Psychological Society (BPS) now has a members' section for **Qualitative** Methods in Psychology (QMiP), which held its inaugural conference in 2008 at the University of Leeds. The section now boasts a membership of more than 1,000 members, making it one of the largest BPS sections. This shows that there is recognition of the need for qualitative research. As Biggerstaff (2012) has argued, the problem with **quantitative** methods is that they leave little room to expand our understanding. If we want to understand depression, for example, and we use (as is often the case) a questionnaire to provide a numerical value of a person's level of depression, what does this tell us about that person's experience of depression or their feelings or emotions.

If we are going to try to understand the motives behind people's behaviour then maybe we need to start asking the right questions, rather than assuming we already know the answers.

Think!

If you wanted to find out whether someone's behaviour was determined by external forces or due to free will, how would you go about studying it? Would you use quantitative or qualitative methods? Would you try to discover the feelings of the individual? Would that be worthwhile? Can we ever know what determines someone's behaviour?

Mini plenary

Using the evaluation points above and the thoughts about studying behaviour you just developed, write a short piece of about 250 words to explain the problems you would have in investigating the influence of free will on behaviour. Consider both the practical and theoretical problems.

A modern debate: criminal responsibility

Most people accept that there are certain circumstances that might push people into crime, e.g. poverty or extreme provocation, etc. Even the courts will accept that the circumstances of the crime and the situation of the individual need to be taken into account, at least when it comes to sentencing and deciding what to do with the criminal. However, this tends to be quite different when it comes to very violent crimes or indeed murder. In these cases, most people are less prepared to accept circumstances as an explanation and tend to favour the view that the person had a choice to do it or not do it.

Modern technology, and in particular brain scanning technology may be changing all that. If we can find enough evidence to show that someone's brain was out of their control and completely determined their behaviour, then maybe we have to accept that they are not responsible for their crime, even if it is murder. Or do we?

New research

A mind of crime: how brain-scanning technology is redefining criminal culpability

Michael Haederle, 23 February 2010, updated 14 June 2017

The question of criminal culpability arose in the case of an admitted murderer named Brian Dugan, where neuroscience and the law collided over whether the evidence provided by prominent neuroscientist Kent Kiehl was enough to show that Dugan should be imprisoned for life rather than executed. The question came down to whether Dugan was completely in control of his behaviour when he raped and killed a 10-year-old girl in 1983. The evidence provided by Kiehl, in the Chicago courtroom, showed that Dugan had abnormally low grey matter density in his brain and that this may have meant that the violence exhibited was as a result of the way his brain had developed, rather than a conscious choice.

Kiehl has been involved in this research for a long time and has interviewed and scanned the brains of more criminals than anyone else in the world. His conclusion is that the brains of some criminals are so different from the norm that it should be considered, not as a question of their guilt, but as a factor when sentencing is being decided. Kiehl told the jury: 'There are abnormalities in his brain function, psychopaths make choices, but those choices are not necessarily informed by emotion in the same way ours are.'

This was the first time that evidence of this kind, based on the use of data collected from an **fMRI** scan, had been used in this way and showed the difficulties that arise when two disciplines, law and neuroscience, which have very different views about human nature, come together in cases such as this.

The view of the law is that people are capable of making choices and as long as it is clear what the consequences of these choices are, then people must accept responsibility for their actions. This view has been established over hundreds of years and is supported by precedents, based on traditional notions of morality and justice.

Neuroscience, on the other hand, is contemporary and constantly responding to changing technology and the data that can be used to change our understanding of human nature, and the ability, or otherwise, of people to make choices. New technologies such as fMRI, **PET** scans and **diffusion tensor studies** have allowed neuroscientists to provide controversial views about how our brains work and what this says about human nature.

One of the most important points arising from this research is that there is no single place in the brain where we can identify the exercise of free will and, as such, we should recognise that the brain involves a range of extremely complex systems that interact with one another to produce a response that is governed more by the laws of physics than the law of the land. This model of behaviour suggests that behaviour is determined, at least to some extent, by forces that are beyond our conscious control.

Following a lengthy court process, costing nearly $1 million, and the need for the jury to be given extra time to deliberate, having initially returned a 10–2 verdict, a unanimous verdict for the death sentence was returned. The defence lawyer, Steve Greenberg, was in the process of launching appeals against some of the rulings made by the judge during the trial, including the decision to not allow the pictures of Dugan's brain, when the death penalty was abolished in the state of Illinois in 2011 and Dugan's sentence was commuted to life imprisonment.

Kiehl argued that it was a terrible waste of money (in this case) but firmly believes that evidence like his will soon be recognised and used regularly in courts so that we can provide a better and more comprehensive justice for those involved in such crimes.

Question time

How does this article contribute to the debate?

Do you think Dugan should have been sentenced to death?

What does this case tell us about criminal responsibility?

What is the way forward?

Chapter plenary

1. What is meant by the term free will?
2. What is meant by the term determinism?
3. What is meant by the term hard determinism?
4. What is meant by the term soft determinism?
5. What is the meant by the term biological determinism?
6. What is meant by the term environmental determinism?
7. What is meant by the term psychic determinism?
8. What is meant by the scientific emphasis on causal explanations?
9. How is humanistic psychology connected to free will?
10. What is Maslow's hierarchy of needs?
11. How is behaviourism connected to determinism?
12. What are Skinner's schedules of reinforcement?
13. What are the benefits of free will?
14. Is free will possible?
15. Is soft determinism a better alternative?
16. What are the limitations of scientific study?
17. Is qualitative research the way forward?
18. Can you provide modern examples of the debate in psychology?

Glossary

Key word	Definition
Biological determinism	The belief that all behaviour is, in the first instance, driven by biological factors (genes, hormones, the nervous system, etc.).
Causal explanations	Based on the belief that we can show cause and effect in behaviour.
Cognitive neuroscience	The section of cognitive psychology that combines the study of brain structures with mental processes.
Determinism	The belief that behaviour does not happen by choice but is instead governed by forces that are beyond our control.
Diffusion tensor studies	The use of magnetic resonance imaging (MRI) and software that uses the diffusion of water molecules to detect contrast in magnetic resonance (MR) images.
Environmental determinism	The belief that all behaviour is the result of some form of conditioning.
fMRI	Stands for functional magnetic resonance imaging and measures brain activity by detecting changes associated with blood flow.
Free will	The ability to make our own choices and decide which option to take from a number of possibilities.
General laws	Explanations that can be applied to all situations.
Hard determinism	The view that we have no free will at all and that all behaviour is driven by uncontrollable forces.
PET	Stands for positron emission tomography and uses a radioactive dye that attaches itself to the active parts of the brain showing which parts are active at certain times.
Positive reinforcer	Something pleasant that is given to encourage a behaviour to be repeated.
Positivist approach	An approach to research that focuses on evidential scientific phenomena.
Psychic determinism	The belief that all behaviour is driven by our unconscious mind.
Qualitative	Non-numerical data that is collected through methods such as observations and interviews.
Quantitative	Numerical data that is collected through such methods as experiments and surveys.
Readiness potential	An electrical brain signal that precedes muscular movement.
Reinforcement	Something that encourages a behaviour to be repeated.

Key word	Definition
Schedules of reinforcement	Different ways of organising the dispensing of rewards to people or animals.
Self-actualisation	The ability to achieve your full potential.
Soft determinism	This is a compromise position between free will and hard determinism. This view suggests that we have a limited range of choices, as most behaviour is decided by some forces, but that it is still possible to make choices on a day-to-day basis.
Zombian	Like a 'zombie', which is a creature that has no control over its behaviour.

Plenary: Exam-style questions and answers with advisory comments

Question 1.

Explain what psychologists mean by free will. [2 marks]

Marks for this question: AO1 = 2

Advice: In a question like this, it's important to make your definition clearly relevant to psychology. This will be helped by the use of a psychological example. There is no need to provide any analysis or evaluation as both of the marks are for AO1: Knowledge and understanding.

Possible answer: Free will is the ability to make our own choices and decide which option to take from a range of possibilities. Humanist psychologists believe that we are all unique and not governed by biological or environmental forces, instead we are free to actively shape our lives.

Question 2.

Sylvie, Astrid and Maureen are discussing their ideal job and why they think they would be good at it. Sylvie thinks she should work in something connected to flying as she has been travelling on planes since she was really little and always loved it. Astrid thinks she should work in something connected to music as 'it's in her DNA'. Maureen says she would love to work with horses as she's always felt a deep connection to them, but she has never known where it came from.

With reference to the section above, outline three different types of determinism in psychology. [6 marks]

Marks for this question: AO2 = 6

Advice: In this question, it's really important to recognise that all the marks are for AO2, which means that you have to show the skill of application to the stem. You will still need to show an understanding of three different types of determinism, but this time by picking out the references to each from the information you have been given. There is still no need to analyse or evaluate.

Possible answer: Environmental determinism suggests that all behaviour is the result of some form of conditioning that you have experienced in your life. This relates to Sylvie as she says she has been travelling on planes since she was little and loved it, so the experience was associated with pleasure. Biological determinism is the belief that all behaviour is driven by biological factors and Astrid says that she thinks music is in her DNA, suggesting that her love for music comes from her biological make-up. Psychic determinism is the belief that behaviour is driven by unconscious forces and Maureen says that she felt she always had a deep connection to horses but never knew where it came from, suggesting an unconscious drive.

Question 3.

Discuss the free will–determinism debate in psychology. Refer to at least two topics you have studied in your answer. **[16 marks]**

Marks for this question: AO1 = 6 and AO3 = 10

Advice: This question is looking for both the skills of knowledge and understanding and those of analysis and evaluation. As there are 6 marks for AO1 and 10 for AO3, there should be greater emphasis on the evaluation. However, all such extended writing questions are marked holistically and therefore it is important that the knowledge is accurate and detailed and that the evaluation is clear and effective.

Possible answer: The free will–determinism debate in psychology is concerned with the extent to which the behaviour of humans is controlled by themselves, and therefore we make free choices or by some other forces that are not under our control and therefore push us towards some behaviour that we have not freely decided.

Free will is something that many people aspire to or already believe they have. It is their ability to make their own decisions, to choose from a range of possibilities that are on offer and to feel as though they are actively shaping their own lives, rather than passive recipients of what is available.

One area of psychology that is most closely associated with free will is humanism, which believes that all humans are unique and not simply a product of their genes or environment. They recognise that there are other forces that influence our behaviour but believe that we are still free to regulate our own behaviour.

Maslow, for example, believed that we need to ensure that our physiological needs are met first, otherwise we starve, but then argues that once these needs are met, we are all striving to achieve our potential and therefore to achieve self-actualisation. As Maslow said, 'What a man can be, he must be', a bit sexist obviously but I'm sure he wasn't deliberately intending to exclude women.

Determinism is the belief that behaviour is driven by forces beyond our control. There are a few versions of this but two of the main ones are hard and soft determinism. Hard determinism is the belief that all of our behaviour is out of our control and therefore we have no free will at all. Soft determinism is more of a compromise between determinism and free will and accepts that most behaviour is out of our control but that we do still make choices, even if the range of possibilities may be limited by our biology or environment.

One area of psychology associated with hard determinism is behaviourism, as Skinner argued that 'free will is an illusion'. This clearly suggests that behaviour is out of our control and in this case driven by environmental forces. According to Skinner, behaviour can be conditioned through the application of tightly controlled schedules of reinforcement whereby we receive rewards for exhibiting certain desirable responses. This approach has many applications, but you may recognise the application of these ideas in schools with the use of merits/house points, etc.

One area of psychology connected to soft determinism is in cognitive psychology as there is the view that our cognition or mental processes enables us to choose from the available options. This has been applied extensively in the area of social learning, where Bandura used the notion of cognitive mediating factors that intervene between the stimulus and response to give people some choice over which behaviour to imitate and which not.

However, cognitive neuroscience has pushed this area further towards the deterministic side with research into the readiness potential. Libet asked participants to note the position of a moving dot as soon as they became consciously aware of their decision to move their finger. Using EEG measurements, he found that there was a gap of 350 milliseconds between their conscious awareness of their decision and the EEG measurement of the brain's preparation to move. This gap marks the period of the readiness potential and suggests that even something as mundane as a finger movement is decided by the brain before we are consciously aware of the decision to do it. This suggests that there may be no middle ground after all.

Bargh and Earp have argued that no matter how positive the benefits of the belief in free will are, a positive illusion is still an illusion. Unfortunately. It is too often the case that a belief in free will is selective in that we take credit for our successes but not for our failures, as shown by many experiments into attribution theory. This seems to point to the idea that belief in free will is more about the management of our self-esteem than it is to do with any real motivation for behaviour.

However, a belief in free will may allow individuals to take credit for their successes and failures, but also to take responsibility for their actions. How can we tell ourselves that effort is the key to success, if we believe that actually it isn't, because we are all merely the product of our genes and environment anyway? How is it possible to change the direction of someone's life if it is already set in stone?

This issue of personal responsibility has become a major talking point in recent years, particularly with advances in brain scanning allowing us to delve deeper into the workings of the criminal mind. Could it be that the responsibility for criminal behaviour lies within the biology of our brains and not within our own minds? Findings from Kiehl/Raine have suggested that the brains of some people may be hard-wired to behave in psychopathic or even murderous ways and this issue became very real in the case of Brian Dugan who raped and killed a 10-year-old girl.

His defence lawyer argued that scans of his brain had identified low levels of grey matter in his brain and this meant (in line with Kiehl/Raine's research) that he lacked the ability to control his behaviour and therefore should be regarded as a psychopath with no control over his behaviour. The jury disagreed and decided that he should be regarded in the same way as any other criminal and he went to jail for life. However, this does highlight an important issue here: are we only exhibiting complete free will when we do something really bad and therefore should we have more and more controls over behaviour in order to create the kind of 'brave new world' envisaged by Huxley and even Skinner.

References

Bargh, J.A. and Earp, B. (2009) The will is caused, not 'free'. *Dialogue: Newsletter of the Society for Personality and Social Psychology*, 24: 13–15.

Biggerstaff, D. (2012) Qualitative research methods in psychology. *Psychology – Selected Papers*. pp. 175–206.

Haederle, M. (2010) A mind of crime. How brain scanning technology is redefining criminal culpability. *Pacific Standard*. 23 February 2010.

Huxley, A. (1998 [1932]) *Brave New World*. London: Vintage. (Originally published by Chatto & Windus.)

Kiehl, K.A. (2006) A cognitive neuroscience perspective on psychopathy: Evidence for paralimbic system dysfunction. *Psychiatry Research*, 142(2–3): 107–128.

Klemm, W.R. (2010). Free will debates: Simple experiments are not so simple. *Advances in Cognitive Psychology*, 6: 47.

Lavazza, A. (2016) Free will and neuroscience: From explaining freedom away to new ways of operationalizing and measuring it. *Frontiers in Human Neuroscience*. 10: 262.

Libet, B., Wright Jr, E.W. and Gleason, C.A. (1983) Preparation- or intention-to-act, in relation to pre-event potentials recorded at the vertex. *Electroencephalography and Clinical Neurophysiology*, 56 (4): 367–372.

Maslow, A.H. (1943). A theory of human motivation. *Psychological Review*, 50 (4): 370–396.

Raine, A. (2013) *The Anatomy of Violence: The Biological Roots of Crime*. New York: Pantheon.

Skinner, B.F. (1965 [1953]) *Science and Human Behavior*. New York: Simon & Schuster. (Originally published by Collier Macmillan.)

Chapter 5
The nature–nurture debate

> **Spec check**
>
> The nature–nurture debate: the relative importance of heredity and environment in determining behaviour; the interactionist approach.

AO1 (Knowledge and understanding): What is the nature–nurture debate?

The nature–nurture debate is one of the oldest debates in psychology. It is something that is commented on by many people on a regular basis, often without realising and certainly without actually referring to the terms nature or nurture themselves. In fact, the terms nature and nurture didn't come into common use until the sixteenth century, but the issue has been hotly debated for hundreds, if not thousands, of years. More recently, Francis Galton coined the term 'nature versus nurture' in the nineteenth century to refer to the debate between those who believe that our genetic inheritance is most important in determining our behaviour and those who believe that all the influences that occur after our birth (or conception) are most important.

> **Question time**
>
> When was the last time you talked about some form of behaviour being either due to external influences (e.g. parents) or due to internal influences (e.g. temperament)? What about that crying baby on the bus/train/plane or in the supermarket or cinema? Didn't you wonder about the kind of parents that might have produced such a 'brat'? Or whether it might just be a difficult child?

What do we mean by nature?

By **nature** we mean all those internal influences that lead to behaviour being pre-determined or **pre-programmed** into us before the environment has had a chance to have an effect. They are sometimes referred to as **innate characteristics** because they are features of our personality that are with us from birth and are therefore part of our biological make-up rather than anything learned in response to our situation. Such features are believed to be **genetic** as they are as much a part of our DNA as our physical characteristics are, such as eye colour or the size of our feet. Therefore, the belief would be that these features are **inherited** from our parents or grandparents in the same way as physical features. How many times have you heard someone say that a person is 'just like their mum or dad' when referring to their mood or temperament?

What do we mean by nurture?

By **nurture** we mean all those external influences that lead to behaviour being **learned** after we have been born/conceived, regardless of any biological characteristics. These types of behaviour will have been formed in response to **environmental influences** that affect our lives on a day-to-day basis and are not constrained by any predetermined physical factors. Therefore, the belief would be that these features are influenced by our **upbringing** and are caused by the way we are treated by parents, friends, teachers and anyone else we come into contact with in the course of our lives. Even the seemingly most individual features of our personalities will have come about due to these influences. How many times have you heard people say, for example, 'it's no wonder they behave like that when they hang round with them'?

The nature–nurture debate therefore refers to the question of which of these is in fact the most important in terms of explaining our behaviour and personality and as such goes to the heart of the question of what we can do to influence or change someone's behaviour. Ultimately, if it's in our nature to behave in certain ways then there's little or nothing we can do, short of genetically modified babies, to change behaviour. Whereas, if it's a part of our nurture, and therefore part of our upbringing, it would have serious implications for the way we raise children in our world.

Question time

Are you more nature or nurture?

Which features of your behaviour do you think are caused by natural influences and which by environmental ones?

Are you more like your mum, dad or someone else in your family?

Do you think this is caused by genetic inheritance or by spending a lot of time with that person?

The relative importance of heredity and environment

If we accept that nature is the deciding factor in the development of our behaviour, we must accept that genes and heredity are of fundamental importance. Whereas, if we accept that nurture is the deciding factor, then we must accept that our behaviour is almost entirely influenced by environmental factors that occur throughout the course of our lives.

However, we may want to consider the possibility that each of these factors has an important role to play and that neither could be regarded as the deciding factor in most, if not all, examples of human behaviour.

Genotype and phenotype

The influence of genes on our characteristics can be seen from the difference between the use of the terms **genotype** and **phenotype**. The genotype is a term used to describe a person's genetic make-up, which is all of the heredity information that we have about that person. Whereas the phenotype is made up of the observed characteristics of that person, e.g. are they tall or short, calm or aggressive, or prone to a particular medical problem?

You could argue that the phenotype is simply the expression of the person's genes, however it would be hard to ignore the likelihood that some or all of the characteristics mentioned above are not influenced by the environment at all.

The interactionist approach

The simplistic aspect of the nature–nurture debate can be very appealing when we are considering the causes of people's behaviour. It provides us with easy explanations, in much the same way that tabloid newspaper articles do, by telling us that the reason for some terribly abhorrent activity that is being reported is caused by being raised badly or by the inherent evil of some group or another.

Such explanations are appealing as they provide not only easy explanations but also easy solutions to whatever problem is being referred to. Inevitably such articles and the associated explanations are flawed as they fail to consider the multitude of factors that lead to these behaviours and how the complex mixture of a range of factors may have come together to produce such behaviour.

This complex mix is what is being referred to in the interactionist approach as the interaction of both natural and nurtural factors, which combine to produce a more complex explanation for behaviour.

In psychopathology, this complex interaction is shown up strongly in the diathesis–stress model of mental illness (see evaluation section, pp. 70–71).

Mini plenary

Draw a line to connect the correct definition with the appropriate term (the first one has been done for you).

Term	Definition
Nurture	Internal influences that lead to behaviour being predetermined before the environment has had a chance to have an effect.
Learned behaviour	The view that behaviour can be explained in terms of heredity and that development occurs in line with the structure of DNA.
Genetic	Behavioural traits that are present at birth and believed to be part of a person's nature.
Innate characteristics	External influences that lead to behaviour being learned after we have been born/conceived, regardless of any biological characteristics.
Environmental influences	Behaviour that has been directly taught or acquired through experience and was not present at birth.
Nature	Features of the external world that my affect our behaviour as we grow and develop, including other people, social situations and experience.

AO2 (Application of knowledge): How does the debate apply in practice?

Nature and the biological approach

To understand how the debate applies to real life, it's useful to go back to the biological approach and the belief that genes and biological structures influence our behaviour. Some would argue that ultimately all behaviour is biological as everything we think and do is related to one biological structure or another. Indeed, in terms of our day-to-day activities, it's hard to get away from the fact that, without these biological structures, we would be unable to do anything.

Interleave me now

The activity of the nervous system
Synaptic transmission and action potential

The nervous system provides a method of communication from the brain to other parts of the body. Communication is made possible through the process of synaptic transmission. **Neurotransmitters** are released into the synapse causing an action potential in the post-synaptic neuron, which allows the message to be relayed.

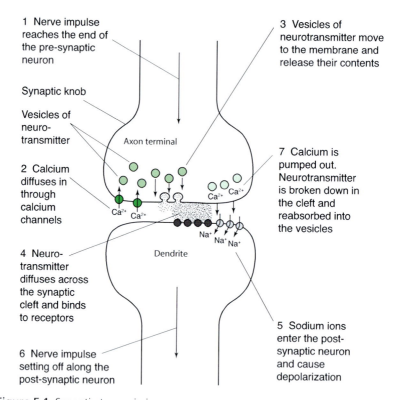

Figure 5.1 Synaptic transmission

Furthermore, the biological approach also contends that our physical characteristics are inherited through our genes and as such, all our characteristic features have been inherited from our parents who have, in turn, inherited their characteristic features from their parents. If we take this to its logical conclusion therefore, it could be seen as a fairly small step to argue that we are born to behave in certain characteristic ways that have ultimately been passed down from our ancestors.

Psychology in real life (AO2 application)

Woman filmed dumping cat in wheelie bin in Coventry

BBC News, 24 August 2010

The RSPCA has said it will be speaking to a woman caught on CCTV dumping a cat into a wheelie bin in Coventry.

Lola, a four-year-old tabby, was discovered 15 hours later by owner Darryl Mann after he heard her cries.

He then checked his security cameras and saw footage of the woman first stroking Lola and then grabbing her by the neck and throwing her in the bin.

Police said they had identified the woman and community support officers had been stationed outside her home.

> **Think!**
>
> How can we explain this behaviour? Is this behaviour genetic? Is it caused by the activity of our nervous system? What is the evolutionary advantage of this behaviour?

If we attempt to understand the behaviour above from a purely biological standpoint then we could apply the activity of the nervous system in this way:

- The woman's brain sent messages to her arm muscles.
- The woman's arm muscles contracted and then relaxed.
- The woman moved one of her arms to pick up the cat and the other to open the bin.
- She dropped the cat into the bin.

Unfortunately, this really, really doesn't explain why she put the cat in the bin, and it would hardly be any kind of defence to say that it was all the fault of her nervous system or indeed her genes.

Her actual explanation? She thought it would be funny! After all, it was only a cat. Maybe, there is a gene for a sick sense of humour? Who knows?

Zuckerman and sensation-seeking

Marvin Zuckerman (1983) has identified a number of biological factors that are related to the personality trait of sensation-seeking. He argues that this trait is different from other traits such as neuroticism or anxiety and that it seems to be related to evolution, genetics and the activity of the nervous system. Sensation-seekers are impulsive and engage in risky activities that are potentially dangerous but can lead to high levels of reward, e.g. gambling. Although, there are many factors related to this trait, such as the dopamine receptor 4 gene, testosterone and high levels of dopamine, Zuckerman argues that a major factor is the enzyme monoamine oxidase (MAO), which functions as a regulator, keeping neurotransmitters in balance. One type of this is specifically related to the regulation of dopamine. Sensation-seekers seem to have low levels of MAO, leading to a lack of regulation, which seems to be particularly prevalent in males and in the young.

> ### Question time
>
> How would Zuckerman have explained the woman's behaviour?
>
> Is it possible that a natural desire for sensation seeking could lead to such behaviour?
>
> If this is a natural behaviour, what could be done to prevent it happening in the future?

Nurture and the behavioural approach

One way of understanding could be to go back to the behaviourist approach and the belief that we are all born as a blank slate, with nothing more than our basic instincts to guide our behaviour. In this situation, it requires a range of environmental experience to understand the range of complex behaviours exhibited by most human beings.

The most fundamental feature of this kind of explanation is that the cause of behaviour lies at the level of stimulus and response (S-R), and that S-R learning can be used to explain most aspects of human behaviour. Classical conditioning, for example, accepts that there are simple reflexive aspects of behaviour, such as the startle response, to situations that may require fight or flight activity, but if we are going to understand how it is that people learn to use this same response in non-threatening situations, such as in the presence of baked beans or cotton wool, then an understanding of the process of learning is required.

Interleave me now

Classical conditioning *involves learning through association*

Pavlov showed how dogs could be conditioned to salivate to the sound of a bell if that bell was sounded repeatedly every time the dogs were given food.

Gradually the dogs learned to associate the sound of a bell (the neutral stimulus, NS) with the food (unconditioned stimulus, UCS) to the point where they would then salivate to just the sound of the bell (conditioned stimulus, CS). (See Figure 5.2.)

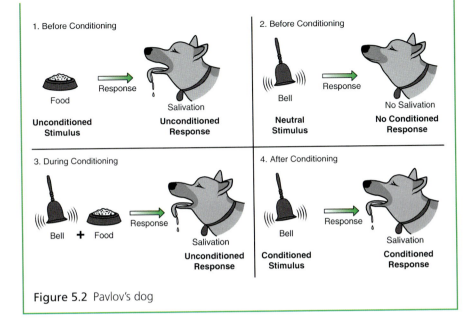

Figure 5.2 Pavlov's dog

Watson and little Albert

John Watson (1920) applied these principles to the study of the development of phobias in a nine-month-old child called Albert. He was able to show how a child with no fear of rats could come to be afraid if the process of classical conditioning was used in a similar way to that outlined above.

Fill in the gaps to show how Albert came to be afraid of the rat in Watson's study.

UCS …… UCR …… ➡ ……   UCS …… + NS …… UCR …… ➡ ……

NS …………… ……………   CS …………… CR ……………

This shows how phobic behaviour can be learned through the process of conditioning.

Top ten phobias

Source: Theta Healing, 19 January 2017 (www.bourgeon.co.uk/top-10-phobias/)
The top 10 phobias people suffer from in the UK include:

1. Fear of spiders (arachnophobia)
2. Fear of heights (acrophobia)
3. Fear of snakes (ophidiophobia)
4. Fear of germs (mysophobia)
5. Fear of public speaking (glossophobia)
6. Fear of needles or getting injections (trypanophobia)
7. Fear of clowns (coulrophobia)
8. Fear of darkness (nyctophobia)
9. Fear of being closed in small spaces (claustrophobia)
10. Fear of crowds (agoraphobia)

Question time

Look at the list of ten of the most common phobias in the UK. How many of them would you say are natural and likely to have been influenced by our desire for survival?

How many would you say are unnatural and likely to be the product of learning and experience? How do you think people become afraid of these?

What makes someone afraid of a tiny spider in a bath? Why do they stay afraid, even when experience should tell them that the spider is harmless?

Classical conditioning might be able show us how certain specific items or situations can come to be associated with fear through the regular pairing of fear with those items or situations and how those experiences may lead someone to produce a fear response, even when there is no actual threat to them.

However, it's harder to explain why the continuing experience of that item/situation leading to no threat doesn't lead to that response becoming extinct in the same way that Pavlov's dogs eventually stopped salivating when food stopped coming at the sound of a bell.

Inevitably, the exact mechanisms involved in this process are considerably more complicated than such a simple examination might allow, but they do, nonetheless, help us to question the usefulness of only considering one side of this debate!

Mini plenary

In what ways might the characteristics listed below be influenced by both genes and environment?

Characteristic	Influenced by genes	Influenced by environment
Height		
Temperament		
Susceptibility to disease		

AO3 (Analysis and evaluation of knowledge): How useful is the nature–nurture debate?

Can we use genes to predict future behaviour?

The question of the usefulness or otherwise of each side of this debate may, to some extent, come down to whether or not we can use either side of it to predict future behaviour.

On the nature side, it may be possible for us to identify a particular genetic variant for intelligence and, having measured the genotype of a baby, then be able to predict the likely IQ of this child in the future. Similarly, if we were to identify an aggressive gene then we should be able to predict the likelihood of that individual becoming a murderer in the future.

However, the problem with this approach is that it's very unlikely that individual genetic variations are responsible for a particular behaviour and it's unknown what the exact combination or number of genes might be to produce such a behaviour.

Behavioural characteristics are complex and likely to be the result of the expression of many genes that work together to produce the basis for a particular behaviour.

The example of criminal behaviour provides a useful reference for this problem. A number of studies (Tiihonen et al., 2015; Caspi et al., 2002) have identified potential genes or indeed gene combinations that are linked to criminal behaviour. Tiihonen et al. examined the genomes of 895 Finnish prisoners who had committed extremely violent crimes, such as homicide, attempted homicide and extremely violent assault. The found that 60 per cent of these individuals had low activity versions of the MAOA gene and the CDH13 gene, compared to 40 per cent of the general population. They concluded that about 5–10 per cent of violent crime could be attributed to this genotype.

What they have not been able to do is to show how these genes work together with other genes in order to produce criminal behaviour in specific individuals. Nor, for that matter, have they been able to show the precise environmental conditions that may need to exist in order for these genes to have the specific effect of crime and/or violence on a particular individual. If you add to that the difficulty of applying these genes to specific crimes, then the possibility of predicting behaviour based on these studies seems highly unlikely.

All of this means that the usefulness of identifying particular genes in order to predict future behaviour is severely limited, not just by the complexities of the specifics of an individual's environment but also by the complex interaction of genes within each individual.

Can we change behaviour by changing the environment?

One of the issues raised concerning the influence of the environment relates to whether changing the environment that an individual is raised in may help to change their future behaviour, regardless of whether we are able to predict the future or not. In many ways this is the basis on which some children are adopted. If we believe the parents to be incapable of providing a suitable environment for the child, then surely by changing the environment, we can change the outcomes for the child.

The problem with this is of course that it assumes that the biggest influence on behaviour is the environment in which a person is raised; yet ignoring the influence of nature means that any attempt to effect some change is likely to fail.

Think!

What are the strengths and weaknesses of adoption studies in psychology?

What evidence is there for nature and/or nurture in these studies?

One of the strengths of adoption studies is that they allow the possibility of comparing an individual's behaviour to that of both their biological parents to look at the influence of genes, and to that of their adoptive parents to look at the influence of the environment. These studies have been conducted in a number of different areas of psychology and the conclusions are somewhat mixed to say the least.

One major area for concern in some cases of adoption these days is related to drug abuse and the removal of children from drug-abusing parents, first and foremost to protect the children but also to remove the possibility that the children will become involved in the same activities.

Research by Kenneth Kendler (2008) and his team, examining 18,000 children and their biological and adoptive parents in Sweden over more than 40 years, showed that the incidence of drug addiction was significantly increased in those individuals who had one biological parent with a drug problem (8.6 per cent) compared with the incidence in the general population (2.9 per cent) born in the same time period.

However, this research also identified a number of factors related to the adoptive home environment that influenced the incidence, including divorce, parental alcoholism and sibling drug abuse. Furthermore, the incidence of drug abuse was also affected by biological parents having a history of alcoholism, major psychiatric illness and criminal convictions. All of which brings into question any direct relationship between the drug use of the biological parents and that of the adopted children (a more detailed discussion of the issues with correlations occurs later in this section, see pp. 72–73).

It seems as though it's impossible to escape the conclusion that it's extremely difficult to separate the effect of nature and nurture. As Kendler states: 'A bad environment can augment the effect of a genetic risk on drug abuse.'

Strengths and weaknesses of the diathesis–stress model

The interactionist approach has led to the development of a diathesis–stress explanation for mental illness. The idea is that genes and environment interact through a process of the genes creating a vulnerability (diathesis) to a particular disorder with the environment providing the trigger (stress) for a particular mental disorder to develop.

This idea has certain strengths, as it's able to show how two individuals exposed to the same environmental stressors may have different reactions depending on their genes and vulnerability. There is plenty of evidence to show that even when people are exposed to exactly the same depressing life events, the reaction of some may be to develop depression whereas in others, the reaction is completely different (La Greca et al., 2013). This could be explained by their genetic vulnerability. In the same way that people who question the connection between smoking and cancer might tell you that grandad smoked 500 cigarettes a day and lived to 150 years old, are failing to understand that some people do not have a genetic vulnerability and yet in another person it may take *significantly* less cigarette smoking or indeed exposure to passive smoking to *significantly* reduce their life expectancy. This model provides a simple solution to the issue of the same events having different outcomes and genetic vulnerability is the key.

However, this model isn't without weaknesses, and it should be noted that what the model doesn't do is to explain the mechanism whereby some people have enough of a trigger to develop the disorder and other people with the same genetic vulnerability do not. Whilst it may be simple to argue that some people have a genetic vulnerability and others do not (although as we have already seen, the ability to identify these genes is far from simple), it is less than simple to explain the level at which stressors have to occur in order for someone to develop depression or indeed any other mental illness. To continue the smoking/cancer analogy, it would be difficult to identify just how many cigarettes/exposure to cigarette smoke would be required in order for someone to develop cancer and even if we were able to do that, we would need to take into account all of the other environmental factors that could be cancer-related and attempt to show how all of these factors combine to cause an individual to develop cancer. This task may be impossible and, as such, the complexities of this type of explanation may make it difficult to apply in anything more than a theoretical manner.

Does epigenetics mean the end of the nature–nurture debate?

Epigenetics is the study of changes in the genetic expression (phenotype) that are passed down to generations but do not involve a change in the DNA sequence (genotype). This is important because it considers the possibility that the kind of experience someone has could bring about a change in their individual behaviour but still be passed on to their offspring. If this is true, it could effectively bring the nature–nurture debate to an end, or, at the very least, bring a third factor to the table meaning that it would no longer be a straight fight between two competing factors.

Epigenetics looks at how influences from the environment trigger biological changes, so changes in diet may lead to chemical tags instructing genes to turn on or off and cause changes that could be relatively minor, such as precise levels of protein used, to extremely serious, such as our susceptibility to disease.

Michael Meaney (2001) has been doing research into epigenetic effects in rats after observing that there are two kinds of rat mothers, those that lick and groom their offspring and those that don't. Meaney and his colleagues found that those baby rats that are licked are more even-tempered and able to cope with stress better than others. When they looked at the epigenome, they found that when a mother licks her pups, she turns on a gene that actually reduces the amount of the stress hormone produced in periods of danger and, furthermore, that this effect was then passed on to the pups who became lickers and groomers themselves.

They had effectively found that there is a link between the experience of maternal care and the expression of genes (in rats at least) and further went on to find that the effect of not having a nurturing mother could be reversed by putting unlicked pups in with nurturing foster mothers or by injecting the rats with a drug trichostatin. This suggests that it's not a question of either nature or nurture but epigenetics all the way!

Question time

What do these findings tell us about the free will vs determinism debate?
Do they leave any room for free will?

Does nature–nurture research show cause and effect?

Research into the effects of nature and nurture has been able to clearly show how certain forms of behaviour are related to biological and environmental factors. Biological research has been able to show clear correlations between family-relatedness and a range of disorders, e.g. Gottesman (1991) has shown how family-relatedness and schizophrenia are linked in such a way that the percentage likelihood of identical twins both developing the disorder is 48 per cent. In a similar review of previous studies, Sideli et al. (2012) have been able to show that child abuse and schizophrenia are related and there is a wealth of evidence to show that there are clear links between abuse in childhood and psychosis.

However, this research is only correlational and therefore only able to suggest a link, rather than a causal relationship. The problem with such research is that is that it merely identifies two events: the experience of child abuse/family-relatedness on the one hand and the development of schizophrenia in later life on the other. This is flawed on two counts: one, because it has failed to isolate the influence of the first event from any other factors that may have occurred in a person's life, and two, because it has failed to provide controlled conditions in which the participant could be exposed to the relevant stimulus and then compared to a control group without the stimulus.

Clearly, neither of these two events could be experimented on in this way and to do so would result in serious ethical implications – and probably a lengthy jail sentence. However, the fact remains that without this level of control or comparison, the researchers may just as well set out to identify the relationship between schizophrenia and shoe size! Who knows what such research would reveal?

As Sideli herself recognises, 'we cannot conclude that the relationship is causal as lack of longitudinal studies prevent us from fully excluding alternative explanations'. Showing that this type of research can do no more than suggest a link and that a cause and effect relationship will have to wait till the time when we can exclude these alternative explanations.

A further issue relates to the percentage likelihoods identified. For Gottesman, this was 48 per cent, which was significantly higher than that for non-identical twins (17 per cent) and for siblings (9 per cent). This suggests that there might be a significant difference, and it could suggest that it is the genes that are the causal factor.

However, it could be argued that if it is the genes that are the causal factor then perhaps the figure should be higher and closer to 100 per cent (identical twins are nearly 100 per cent identical) in order to more clearly show that genes are the cause and that if this is not achieved then maybe the finding is not significant at all. But perhaps this is too demanding and the possibility of achieving a perfect +/–1 correlation coefficient is nearly impossible, so maybe we should consider what correlation coefficient we are prepared to accept. Would we accept 80 per cent, as 0.8 is considered to be a strong correlation coefficient?

All of which leads to the need to treat correlational studies with 'significant' caution or run the risk of attributing cause to something where none is demonstrably present.

Mini plenary

In the table below, identify an evaluation point in the section on the left. Tick the appropriate box to show whether the point supports nature, nurture, neither or both; and then in the section on the right, explain why.

Evaluation point	Nature	Nurture	Neither	Both	Explanation
Can we use genes to predict future behaviour?		{tick}			Supports nurture because it shows the problems associated with using genes to explain behaviour

A modern debate: born to be trans?

The nature–nurture debate constantly throws up areas for discussion as to the likely causes of behaviour. One such modern discussion has arisen over the question of whether transgender individuals are born that way or made that way through the influence of their upbringing.

New research

Transgender people are born that way, according to a new study

Pink News: Josh Jackman, 15 March 2018
A new discovery from the University of São Paulo's Medical School has suggested that the brains of **transgender** and **cisgender** adults are significantly different.

Spizzirri et al. (2018) found that the insula region of the brain (a section of the cerebral cortex) had less volume in trans people than cis people. This research is regarded as significant as the insula is important for self-awareness, empathy and body image.

The main author of the study, Giancarlo Spizzirri, suggested that the findings indicated that people may actually be trans inside the womb, rather than developing it after birth. 'We found that trans people have characteristics that bring them closer to the gender with which they identify and their brains have particularities, suggesting that the differences begin to occur during gestation,' he said in a statement.

This has led researchers at the university to argue that the study shows that being trans is not a product of society but actually refers to a natural difference between trans and cis people and not just something that is down to behavioural differences. Others at the university have argued that it's not possible to show a direct link with transgender but the fact that the difference is there is 'relevant'.

An associate researcher at the university, Geraldo Busatto, suggests that the finding is important because body image is a significant aspect of the issues faced by trans people and therefore differences in this region of the brain may help us to understand the issue better and prevent some of the discrimination and persecution suffered by trans people. The day before the research went public, anti-trans activists had been involved in protests at the UK parliament calling for an end to the 'trend of fashionable transgenderism'.

Question time

How does this article relate to the nature–nurture debate?

What do you think is meant by the phrase 'fashionable transgenderism'?

What might be the ethical implications of believing either one or the other side of this debate?

What is the alternative to being on one side or the other? Is it possible to do this?

Chapter plenary

1. What is meant by the term nature?
2. What are the influences on our nature?
3. What is meant by the term nurture?
4. What are the influences on our nurture?
5. What is the difference between genotype and phenotype?
6. What is the interactionist approach?
7. Which psychological approach is linked to nature?
8. Which research shows the influence of nature on behaviour?
9. Which psychological approach is linked to nurture?

10. Which research shows the influence of nurture on behaviour?

11. How do nature and nurture work together to influence human behaviour. Give examples.

12. What evidence is there about whether we can use genes to predict future behaviour?

13. What evidence is there about whether we can change behaviour by changing the environment?

14. What are the strengths and weaknesses of the diathesis–stress model?

15. What evidence is there to suggest that epigenetics means the end of the nature–nurture debate?

16. Does nature–nurture research show cause and effect?

17. Can you provide examples of the nature–nurture debate in modern society?

18. What are the ethical issues concerning the nature–nurture debate?

Glossary

Key word	Definition
Cisgender	Having a gender identity or expression that matches your assigned sex.
Classical conditioning	Learning through association in which a previously neutral, environmental stimulus is paired with a naturally occurring stimulus until the environmental stimulus brings about the same response as the natural stimulus.
Environmental influences	Features of the external world that my affect our behaviour as we grow and develop, including other people, social situations and experiences.
Epigenome	A number of chemical compounds that tell the genome what to do. They modify the genome without altering the DNA sequence but have a role in deciding which genes are active.
Genetic	The view that behaviour can be explained in terms of heredity and that development occurs in line with the structure of DNA.
Genotype	A person's genetic make-up, which is all of the heredity information that we have about that person.
Inherited	Refers to the passing of characteristics from parents and ancestors. At birth, a person will have 50 per cent of each parent's genes.
Innate characteristics	Behavioural traits that are present at birth and believed to be part of a person's nature.
Learned	Behaviour that has been directly taught or acquired through experience and was not present at birth.

Key word	Definition
Nature	Internal influences that lead to behaviour being pre-determined before the environment has had a chance to have an effect.
Neurotransmitters	Chemical messengers that send information between neurons after being released into a synapse, e.g. serotonin and dopamine.
Nurture	External influences that lead to behaviour being learned after we have been born/conceived, regardless of any biological characteristics.
Phenotype	The observable characteristics of a person, resulting from the interaction of their genotype with their environment.
Pre-programmed	A person's behaviour that has been set in advance such that their responses will be automatic without the need of external control or influence.
Transgender	Having a gender identity or expression that differs from your assigned sex.
Upbringing	Refers to the way a child is raised, and all of the treatment and instruction received by a child from their parents/carers.

Plenary: Exam-style questions and answers with advisory comments

Question 1.

What is meant by the nature–nurture debate in psychology? [2 marks]

Marks for this question: AO1 = 2

Advice: In a question like this, it's important to make sure you are outlining the debate rather than just what is meant by nature and what is meant by nurture. Although you will still need to show an understanding of this to get both marks. There is no need to provide any analysis or evaluation as both of the marks are for AO1: Knowledge and understanding.

Possible answer: The debate refers to the question of how much of our behaviour is governed by internal influences that are present at birth, such as genes, and how much of our behaviour is governed by external influences, such as the experiences that we have throughout our life.

Question 2.

Syd and Ali are discussing the fact that both of them are terribly afraid of dogs. Syd puts it down to a bad experience he had when he was a child and a dog bit him. Ali can't remember having had any bad experiences and thinks that maybe he was just born that way because his dad has the same problem.

With reference to the section above, identify the influence of nature on our behaviour and the influence of nurture on our behaviour. [2 marks]

Marks for this question: AO2 = 2

Advice: In this question, it's really important to recognise that both marks are for AO2, which means that you have to show the skill of application to the stem. You will still need to show an understanding of nature and nurture, but this time by picking out the references to each from the information you have been given. There is still no need to analyse or evaluate.

Possible answer: Nurture is suggested by Syd because he relates it to a bad experience 'a dog bit him'. Nature is suggested by Ali as he suggests that it's not due to experience but just being born that way and, therefore, possibly genetic as 'his dad has the same problem'.

Question 3.

Discuss the nature–nurture debate in psychology. Refer to at least two topics you have studied in your answer. [16 marks]

Marks for this question: AO1 = 6 and AO3 = 10

Advice: This question is looking for both the skills of knowledge and understanding and those of analysis and evaluation. As there are 6 marks for AO1 and 10 for AO3, there should be greater emphasis on the evaluation. However, all such extended writing questions are marked holistically and therefore it is important that the knowledge is accurate and detailed and that the evaluation is clear and effective.

Possible answer: The nature–nurture debate in psychology is concerned with the extent to which the behaviour of humans and animals is pre-programmed, and therefore present at birth, or the result of environmental influence, and therefore constantly changing due to life experiences.

The debate has a long history within the area of philosophy but has come to prominence in psychology due to the fact that different approaches in psychology have very different views about the influence of each of these factors.

The nature side of the debate is closely related to the biological approach in psychology and, as a consequence, focuses on the influence of genes, hormones and the nervous system. The influence of genes would suggest that our behaviour is inherited in the same way as other (physical) characteristics, and therefore any variation in behaviour would be due to gene variation thus explaining aggression, IQ and even sexuality. As genes would determine the structure and activity of our brain, the activity of our nervous system and hormones would also be affected and therefore any variations in these would also be predetermined from inherited genes, e.g. high levels of dopamine, which have been associated with sensation-seeking and mental disorders such as schizophrenia and have been linked to specific genes and enzymes by Zuckerman, Gottesman and others.

The nurture side of the debate is closely related to the behaviourist approach and the notion that all behaviour is learned. From this point of view, behaviour is learned through a process of conditioning that involves associations being made between environmental stimuli and behavioural responses, e.g. 'Little Albert'.

Whilst it is true to say that the debate can sometimes be as polarised as this, most researchers take a more interactionist approach and consider the relative importance of both sides of the debate. This suggests that either the two have an equal impact on behaviour or, more often, that whilst one might have more of an impact, it isn't possible to completely discount the effect of the other and that most behaviour is influenced by both in at least some way. This is shown most clearly in the diathesis–stress model of mental illness, which proposes that some individuals may have a genetic vulnerability to that disorder (diathesis) but that an environmental trigger (stress) is required in order to set it off.

Whilst the diathesis–stress model does have significant strengths in its ability to show how different outcomes can result from the same events, e.g. highly significant life events such as child abuse or natural disasters may lead some to develop depression or other mental disorders, whilst others without the genetic vulnerability do not. It also has problems because it is difficult to identify the exact level of disturbance that is likely to cause one person with the vulnerability to suffer when another person with the same gene does not and furthermore, it is difficult to say whether it is one gene or a combination of genes that leads to this effect.

This leads on to another problem in this area, which is the problem of causality. It is difficult to provide experimental evidence to show the influence of either side of this debate, particularly when working with sensitive issues such as mental illness and child abuse. Consequently, much of the research in this area tends to be correlational and therefore provides no more than a link between such factors. Research by Sideli et al. has shown that there is a link between child abuse and schizophrenia, but Sideli recognises that just because there is a link doesn't mean that the one causes the other. As she herself has said, 'we cannot conclude that the relationship is causal as lack of longitudinal studies prevent us from fully excluding alternative explanations'. This shows that we cannot show cause and effect from such research until we are able to rule out all other possible variables that could have caused the problem, which is more or less impossible.

Advances in the study of genetics may have dealt a final blow to the nature–nurture debate with research into the role of epigenetics in behaviour. Epigenetic research has looked into the possibility that life experiences could change the phenotype of an organism without altering their genotype but still be passed down through generations. Research by Meaney on rats, looking into the effects of having mothers who licked their pups regularly, showed how the effect of this behaviour was to turn on genes that helped the baby rats cope with stress, and that this behaviour could be passed on to future generations without affecting the genotype of these individuals. This is extremely important as it suggests that the whole idea of seeing nature and nurture as separate entities is flawed – and that, in fact, they are so closely linked as to almost be inseparable.

One final point worth considering is the ethical implications of this research, as many of the topics that are affected by this debate are socially sensitive, e.g. whether transgenderism is learned or innate. In some ways, whatever the conclusion of this discussion, it may lead to problematic outcomes, although it is certainly true that psychologists have a duty not to back away from difficult discussions if they are going to make progress.

References

Caspi, A., McClay, J., Moffitt, T.E., Mill, J., Martin, J., Craig, I.W., Taylor, A. and Poulton, R. (2002) Role of genotype in the cycle of violence in maltreated children. *Science*, 297 (5582): 851–854.

Gottesman, I.I. (1991) *Schizophrenia Genesis: The Origins of Madness*. New York: W.H. Freeman, Times Books, Henry Holt & Co.

Kendler, K.S., Schmitt, E., Aggen, S.H. and Prescott, C.A. (2008) Genetic and environmental influences on alcohol, caffeine, cannabis, and nicotine use from early adolescence to middle adulthood. *Archives of General Psychiatry*, 65 (6): 674–682.

La Greca, A.M., Lai, B.S., Joormann, J., Auslander, B.B. and Short, M.A. (2013) Children's risk and resilience following a natural disaster: Genetic vulnerability, posttraumatic stress, and depression. *Journal of Affective Disorders*, 151 (3): 860–867.

Meaney, M.J. (2001) Maternal care, gene expression, and the transmission of individual differences in stress reactivity across generations. *Annual Review of Neuroscience*, 24 (1): 1161–1192.

Sideli, L., Mule, A., La Barbera, D. and Murray, R.M. (2012) Do child abuse and maltreatment increase risk of schizophrenia? *Psychiatry Investigation*, 9 (2): 87.

Spizzirri, G., Duran, F.L.S., Chaim-Avancini, T.M., Serpa, M.H., Cavallet, M., Pereira, C.M.A., Santos, P.P., Squarzoni, P., da Costa, N.A., Busatto, G.F. and Abdo, C.H.N. (2018). Grey and white matter volumes either in treatment-naïve or hormone-treated transgender women: A voxel-based morphometry study. *Scientific Reports*, 8 (1): 736.

Tiihonen, J., Rautiainen, M.R., Ollila, H.M., Repo-Tiihonen, E., Virkkunen, M., Palotie, A., Pietiläinen, O., Kristiansson, K. et al. (2015) Genetic background of extreme violent behavior. *Molecular Psychiatry*, 20 (6): 786.

Watson, J.B. and Rayner, R. (1920) Conditioned emotional reactions. *Journal of Experimental Psychology*, 3: 1–14.

Zuckerman, M. (ed.) (1983) *Biological Bases of Sensation Seeking, Impulsivity, and Anxiety*. Lawrence Erlbaum Associates.

Chapter 6
Holism and reductionism

Spec check

Holism and reductionism. Levels of explanation in psychology. Biological reductionism and environmental (stimulus response) reductionism.

AO1 (Knowledge and understanding): What is the basis of the holism–reductionism debate?

The holism–reductionism debate is one of those debates that comes down to whether you want to look for the simplest explanation for something or the most complex explanation. The simplest explanation would seek to find a single cause for examples of behaviour so that we could test that explanation more easily, that is **reductionism**. Whereas, the most complex explanation would try to look at the complete picture to explain behaviour and explore all of the factors that might influence it, that is **holism**.

Where does the idea of holism come from?

The idea of holism has a long history dating back to the ancient Greeks. Aristotle used the term 'holos' in his book *Metaphysics* to refer to the notion that 'the whole is more than the sum of its parts'. Therefore, we cannot understand the nature of something unless we take into account the social, mental and economic factors as well as the physical, chemical and biological. In fact, it is the whole that determines how the component parts behave rather than the other way round.

This idea was taken up by **Gestalt** psychologists in the early part of the twentieth century and relates to seeing things as a 'whole form' rather than as a collection of parts. This view became very influential within the field of perception and helped to create laws that could explain how we come to give seemingly separate components whole forms, for example through laws such as proximity whereby individual people standing close to one another might be regarded as a group rather than as separate individuals.

Seeing a person as a whole form, rather than being made up of separate cells or chemical processes, is useful for providing a complete explanation as it takes into account all of the factors exerting pressure on the individual to prevent simplistic explanations that only focus on one factor, e.g. biochemistry.

Where does reductionism come from?

Reductionism is an attempt to explain behaviour in its simplest possible terms, focusing on just one of the factors identified by Aristotle above, e.g. to understand behaviour you could purely focus on the biochemical factors that cause it.

The idea of reductionism also began in ancient Greece but was later taken up by Descartes who argued that the way to understand a complex phenomenon was to break it down, step by step, into simpler processes, which can help to show its formation.

This is related to the notion of **parsimony**, which is based on the view that the simplest explanation is often the best. The explanation that relies on the fewest possible variables allows us to isolate one and decide that it is the cause. The advantages of this for a scientific method should be obvious, as not only does this allow us to identify single causes for behaviour but also, if we are looking to change or treat these behaviours, having a single cause is most likely to provide us with a single treatment.

What is the difference between biological reductionism and environmental (stimulus–response) reductionism?

If you were asked to explain what makes people do the things they do, you might well give two different types of explanation: one might refer to the biological mechanisms that make up human behaviour, and so you might talk about genes, neurons, neurotransmitters, hormones and brain structure; the other might refer to environmental factors that influence human behaviour, so you might talk about how people respond to a stimulus from the environment, e.g. you stub your toe, you swear.

Biological reductionism

Reducing human behaviour down to its most basic biological components might involve an examination of the genetic structure of human beings, trying to show that we have genes that are inherited from our parents and go some way to explaining both our physical and psychological characteristics. From these genes we have a nervous system that enables cells to communicate with our muscles, sending messages with instructions on what to do. This happens through the process of **synaptic transmission** in which cells communicate with one another using **neurotransmitters**. Another part of this is the **endocrine system** through which **hormones**, that affect our behaviour over a prolonged period of time, are released into the bloodstream. Alongside this, our brain has different structures that appear to be responsible for certain forms of behaviour and, if damaged, affect our ability to demonstrate that behaviour.

All of this shows, from a biological reductionist point of view, that in order to understand behaviour we have to understand the biological process that makes it happen.

Environmental (stimulus–response) reductionism

Human behaviour does not occur in isolation from our environment, in fact quite the opposite, it occurs in response to stimuli from the environment. If we are going to understand human behaviour, we have to see it in this way – something happens, and we react to that. Without the stimulus, there would be no response, without an environment to react to, there would be no behaviour.

From birth, our environment is affecting us. All the experiences we encounter affect us and help to guide our behaviour. These experiences shape our behaviour with the result that we become conditioned to behave in these ways throughout our lives. From this we can see that our behaviour can be broken down into **conditioned reactions** that can be explained with reference to learning.

> **Think!**
>
> What about your own behaviour? Could you take an example of your behaviour and say, for example, that I do this because of this one thing? What about eating? Do you only eat when you have a biological need?

Levels of explanation

At the start of this section, I talked about the difference between simple and complex explanations for human behaviour. In a similar way, we can talk about there being different **levels of explanation**, with the simplest levels at the bottom and the most complex levels at the top. However, this may not go quite the way you think as the more scientific the explanation, the simpler the explanation becomes and logically the lower the level it is. Consequently, the less scientific, the more complex and the higher the level. Consider the diagram shown in Figure 6.1.

What can be inferred from this is that the higher the level of explanation, the more holistic is the explanation as it involves ever more complex and, some would say, obscure aspects of understanding. Whereas, the lower the level of explanation,

Different levels of behaviour

Sociology
Psychology
Biology
Chemistry
Physics

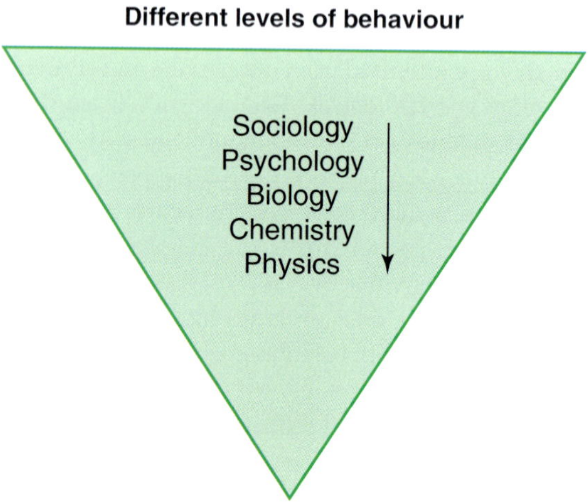

Figure 6.1 Levels of explanation

the more reductionist is the explanation, as it involves ever less complex structures and processes, which are based on concrete aspects of understanding.

It also follows that the more holistic an explanation becomes, the less open to **objective** testing and less scientific it becomes; and the more reductionist an explanation becomes, the more open to objective testing and the more scientific it becomes. In fact, one of the goals of science is to be able to reduce explanations down to as few different variables as possible so that we can find a single cause.

This may explain why so few approaches in psychology would be referred to as holistic!

Question time

Which discipline has the highest level of explanation and which the lowest?
Is this what you expected? Why?
What does this say about whether reductionism is a good or a bad thing?
Has this changed the way you think about reductionism?

Mini plenary

Write a short summary of the information above. It should answer the following questions.

What is meant by holism? What is meant by reductionism? What is the difference between biological reductionism and environmental (stimulus–response) reductionism? What is meant by levels of explanation?

AO2 (Application of knowledge): How does the debate apply in practice?

Interleave me now

Holism and the humanist approach

Carl Rogers was one of the most influential psychologists of the twentieth century and one of the founders of the humanist approach. He believed that in order to understand human behaviour, we needed to take psychology out of the lab and away from the study of animals.

The focus of Rogers's (1951) work is on the whole person, what he refers to as the '**fully functioning person**'. In order to achieve this level of functioning, it is important first to have an openness to experience, not to be closed off in approach. Inevitably, this leads to a rejection of methods that tend towards narrowing down the causes of human behaviour, and instead a movement towards methods that open up a range of possibilities. Therefore, the focus is going to be on qualitative methods, rather than quantitative, as they provide such opportunities to really explore the depth of human behaviour and experience.

The person-centred approach

Rogers' approach was to put human beings at the centre of his work and to focus on what it is that leads to a better understanding of human life. From this he believed that people could be guided towards 'the good life', which is one that accepts all of the possibilities that life can offer and is not for the 'faint-hearted' as, in Rogers' words, 'It involves the courage to be. It means launching oneself fully into the stream of life' (Rogers, 1961).

Central to this is an understanding of 'the self' and the needs of individual people. In order to understand how people become psychologically maladjusted we need to understand how their notion of self becomes inconsistent with their aspirations. In other words, when a person starts to see themselves as distant from their ideal self, they may feel psychologically disordered in some way.

From this Rogers developed client-centred therapy, which has empathy built in as one of its core principles. In order to be able to help a person become psychologically adjusted the therapist needs to show empathetic understanding of the individual.

Psychotherapy is based around a conversation between the client and the therapist in which the therapist must provide:

- **Genuineness**
- **Empathy**
- **Unconditional positive regard**

The aim of therapy is to increase the feelings of **self-worth** within the client and return the client to a state of congruence in which there is a closer match between their perceived self and their ideal self. Once this is achieved, the client can become a fully functioning person.

Reductionism and biopsychology

Recent developments in brain scanning have made it possible to identify the parts of the brain involved in a range of human behaviours that previously could have only been identified **post-mortem**. This has meant that often small areas of the brain can be studied and shown to be related to some fairly complex human behaviour.

Interleave me now
Ways of studying the brain

The complexity of the brain is very difficult to study and, even in the recent past, we could only get an idea of the structure of the brain from CAT scans and the like. Technology has advanced considerably, and this has enabled us to obtain more information about the activity of the brain, giving us a much clearer idea of which parts of the brain are responsible for which behaviours.

Functional Magnetic Resonance Imaging (fMRI)

This works with a magnetic field and pulses of radio wave energy to provide us with pictures that can be interpreted to identify activity in specific areas of the brain. It works by detecting changes in blood flow that occur in the active areas of the brain. When there is neural activity in a certain part of the brain, it consumes more oxygen and, to enable this to happen, blood flow is directed to that area of the brain. That can be picked up by the scanner, which produces 3D images (with colour added to indicate levels of activity) that enable us to develop a map of the parts of the brain associated with different activities.

Psychology in real life (AO2 application)

Human behaviour: is it all in the brain – or the mind?

Neuroimaging is widely regarded as the key to understanding everything we do, but Sally Satel and Scott O. Lilienfeld, the authors of a controversial book, *Brainwashed*, published in 2013, claim this approach is misguided and dangerous.

There is a common trend in the modern age to provide images of the brain alongside headlines indicating that the image shows how the brain looks when you're in love or angry or maybe even thinking of killing someone! The media and neuroscientists both seem to want to show us that there are neural foundations to all forms of behaviour, from our devotion to our iphones to an obsession with self-tanning.

Satel and Lilienfeld argue that the belief that the brain is the last scientific frontier may well be justified, but the kind of attitude that goes alongside this, with its moral superiority, suggesting that anyone who doesn't agree with this just doesn't understand, could be described as **neurocentrism**. This is the view that human behaviour can be exclusively explained with reference to the brain, a view that has been massively boosted by the ability to display ever more sophisticated images of the brain at work.

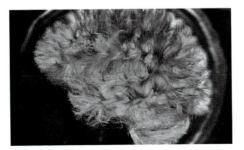

Figure 6.2 'Ephemeral and mysterious': an image of a brain from the Human Connectome Project. Courtesy of V.J. Wedeen and L.L. Wald, Martinos Center, Harvard University, California.

> **Think!**
>
> What do Satel and Lilienfeld mean by 'neurocentrism'? How does this relate to the holism–reductionism debate?
>
> What other factors might be involved in the obsession with self-tanning/iPhones, etc.?

> **Mini plenary**
>
> In the exams, you will be required not only to identify points of application, but also to be able to explain them. Try this for yourself, by finishing the sentences below:
>
> The person-centred approach in humanism is holistic because …
>
> Neuroimaging is reductionist because …

AO3 (Analysis and evaluation of knowledge): How useful is the holism–reductionism debate?

Does holism tell us more or less?

Holism seems to offer the opportunity to explain more about a person's behaviour than we previously knew. The human mind tends to try to make sense of information and in doing so often presents us with a bigger, clearer picture than was the case before. One of the best examples of this is in the study of perception, where Gestalt laws help us to understand what we are seeing better than we would if we were merely seeing things as individual parts. In fact, one of the difficulties for people with autism spectrum disorder is that they struggle to see things as a whole, which might indicate the importance of doing so for a better understanding of the things that we see. One example of how holism helps is in the Gestalt law of closure, which allows us to see something as a whole even if we can't see the whole thing. This is linked to our survival as we don't need to see the whole of a predator in order to recognise it and therefore avoid danger more quickly.

However, a problem with the way that the mind tries to make sense of things is that sometimes it distorts the things that we see and therefore we end up either seeing things that aren't there or possibly just seeing them in ways that are not quite right. For example, in our desire to avoid predators, we may see something that resembles a predator, e.g. a couple of tree trunks might resemble the legs of an animal, and we could end up running away from a tree!

What are the benefits of reductionism?

As mentioned earlier, a reductionist approach fits with the aims of science and does allow for a more scientific approach. One of the aims of science is to test hypotheses and, in order to do this best, it is beneficial to have a clear idea of how one variable affects behaviour, rather than having lots of possibilities with each one being dependent on the other. In order to identify a cause of behaviour rather than just a possible relationship, scientists benefit from being able to show that one factor causes certain forms of behaviour to occur.

An example of this is in the field of environmental reductionism and the stimulus–response approach. If we are able to change people's behaviour with the use of association between a particular stimulus and a specific response, then this opens up lots of possibilities. In his work with rats, Skinner (1965 [1953]) was able to use negative reinforcement to get the rats to press a lever by shining a yellow light just before the floor of their cage became electrified. If the rat pressed the lever quickly enough, it could avoid the shock. Similarly, speed cameras work by inducing the same lever (brake) pressing behaviour whenever you see a big yellow box by the side of the road, thus preventing many accidents. It is a very simplistic procedure, but it works as drivers will respond to it without the need for a holistic understanding, simply because they have learned to associate that stimulus with a particular response.

Unfortunately, it may only work when the big yellow box is present and not be generalised, therefore the benefits are situation-specific and don't deal with the whole problem of people driving too fast.

Can reductionist approaches work with human behaviour?

Reductionism clearly works well with the physical sciences such as physics and maths, which allow for highly objective testing, as the material and concepts they are working with tend to be very concrete and lend themselves more easily to manipulation and testing. However, human beings are somewhat less open to manipulation and, as such, objective testing becomes somewhat more difficult.

While applying a certain force to a certain object in exactly the same conditions may lead to that object travelling the same distance each time, doing the same thing to a human being may lead a variety of results. If you were to push the person sitting next to you, it is quite uncertain what their response would be and there may be a variety of factors that affect their reaction, many of which would be difficult to have knowledge of before you did your test. Human beings are not objects, and therefore their behaviour is somewhat less predictable than that of objects being manipulated in a lab.

An example of this is in the Reicher and Haslam (2006) replication of Zimbardo's Stanford Prison Experiment, in which they created the same stimulus, but which led to a very different response from the original, possibly due to the very different characters involved in the study.

Therefore, it isn't always easy to predict which way your research will go, as sometimes humans throw a spanner in the works and decide to do things their own way.

Is holism the ultimate interactionist approach?

In most of the debates that we look at in psychology, there is an interactionist alternative that provides a kind of halfway point between the two sides of the debate and incorporates a little bit of each side so as to come to a compromise position between the two. In the nature–nurture debate we are able to come to a compromise and accept that it is a bit of each. In the free will–determinism debate, we are also able to recognise that there could be mixture of the two, which comes from the idea of soft determinism.

However, in this debate, you could argue that holism *is* that mixture because it accepts that there are biological and environmental variables that affect our behaviour, but it also suggests that there is a range of other variables that can give a fuller explanation if taken into account, and that, therefore, a compromise is not needed as we already have one.

But this is not quite true, as pointed out by Lundh (2015), who argues that holism and **interactionism** are not the same thing, as holism tends to focus on all parts of a whole system because it believes it's impossible to separate them, whereas interactionism looks at how specific parts interact with one another. Interactionism is therefore more concerned with causality as it attempts to identify how certain parts interact to explain the cause of some form of behaviour or issue.

For example PKU is an inherited disorder that involves the unhealthy build-up of an amino acid whenever the person consumes food high in protein. In order to prevent this happening, a child can be screened shortly after birth and, if PKU is detected, they can be placed on a low protein diet that will prevent this from being a major problem. This is a clear case of the interaction between genes and environment but not, strictly speaking, holistic, as it involves very few factors interacting rather than a whole range of them, which might be the case with a holistic explanation.

Is holism the way forward with mental disorders?

Holistic approaches in the field of mental disorders are regarded as a useful way of dealing with problems that are often **multifaceted** and too complex to simply explain in terms of biological mechanisms.

Indeed, in relation to the disorder of depression, it is hard to see that a simplistic notion of low levels of **serotonin** provides an explanation for why someone is suffering the crippling effects of depression. It is also possible to argue that the fact that serotonin levels are low is as much an effect of the depression as a cause and, as such, treating the symptoms of a disorder does not get to the root cause; and if you only treat the symptoms, you run the risk of symptom substitution and all the problems that arise from that.

A holistic approach, on the other hand, would allow us to develop an understanding of the range of issues faced by this person, which are as likely to be related to their circumstances and relationships as they are to their biological functioning. Consequently, being able to analyse a person both subjectively and objectively might give us a better insight into their problems.

Rogers' person-centred approach allowed this level of analysis to occur and provide a fuller understanding of the problems encountered by an individual. When dealing with issues of self-worth, it is hard to find completely objective reasons for why an individual may be experiencing low self-worth, particularly when a simple analysis of their lives might lead to the objective view that an individual who appears to be successful should not be depressed.

The problem is that when you only focus on individual trees or, indeed, branches of the tree, you can miss what is actually going on in the whole forest or the rest of the tree. Unfortunately, though, if you don't deal with the rotting branch soon enough, you might find that you lose the whole tree, so a reductionist approach may be necessary, at least in the short term. Maybe this is where reductionist approaches work best, by providing a temporary fix while you try to deal with the whole problem. Therefore, in the field of mental health, drugs may be necessary for today while more holistic approaches can be used for tomorrow and the day/week/month after.

Mini plenary

In the table below, identify an evaluation point in the section on the left. Tick the appropriate box to show whether the point supports holism or reductionism and then in the section on the right, explain why.

Evaluation point	Holism	Reductionism	Explanation

A modern debate: holistic medicine, complete care or complete nonsense?

In recent times, the question of the best way to treat illness has been thrown into confusion by the rise of more traditional methods of treatment. These methods offer the opportunity to treat the whole person, rather than just a specific problem or ailment. As such, it has become known as 'holistic medicine'.

New research

Does holistic medicine work?

Nathan Cranford, 13 March 2014

There has been a shift towards 'holistic' medicine in the US, in spite of the fact that life expectancy has doubled in the last century, partially as a result of a growing distrust of the pharmaceutical industry, as some people believe that they are acting in the interests of profit rather than in the interests of health.

The goal of holistic medicine is not simply to treat the body but to treat the mind, body and soul. This involves a range of approaches, from homeopathy to acupuncture, that can be used to treat a variety of conditions, from cancer to headaches. The belief is that all illnesses are the result of an imbalance between the three areas of mind, body and soul, and that restoring that balance will return the person to good health. Consequently, meditation is preferred to medication.

Holistic approaches incorporate those treatments also referred to as 'alternative' or 'complimentary'. However, there is an important difference between the two, as complimentary medicine is just that as it is intended to be used alongside other medication, whereas alternative, as the name suggests, is used as a substitute for traditional medication.

As suggested earlier, one of the reasons that people use holistic approaches is because they believe the pharmaceutical industry is just in it to make money, regardless of the health of the public. However, the same could be said of holistic approaches, which could be accused of giving people false hope with products that provide no real benefit except in lining the pockets of those who are selling them. Opponents of these approaches argue that they lack the peer review process that traditional medicines are subject to, and usually they rely on anecdotal evidence of claims from individuals that they used the holistic approach and got better. The problem with this is that the patient in these cases may well have got better anyway, given time, and that the apparent cure might just be due to a placebo effect. If the medicine used actually did work, it would no longer be dubbed holistic as it would just be another form of medicine!

Apart from those that distrust the pharmaceutical industry, other people attracted to this form of medicine are those who want to take a certain amount of control over their own health, and holistic medicine is certainly more patient-centred than the traditional approach. However, it may also be giving false hope to people who are unable to cope with the reality of their illness, especially in the case of those with a terminal diagnosis.

The conclusion of the article is that natural remedies do have a place in medical care, as many involve people leading a more healthy lifestyle, which would certainly be encouraged by doctors. However, the final conclusion is that if you want to keep the doctor away, it's probably best to the listen to the advice of an actual doctor.

Question time

How does this article relate to the holism–reductionism debate?

Why do you think there is a growing distrust of the pharmaceutical industry?

What are the problems with holistic medicine, as identified above?

What is an alternative to being on one side or the other of a debate? Is it possible to do it in this case?

Chapter plenary

1. What is the basis of the holism–reductionism debate?
2. Where does the idea of holism come from?
3. Where does the idea of reductionism come from?
4. What is biological reductionism?
5. What is environmental (stimulus–response) reductionism?
6. What is the difference between biological reductionism and environmental (stimulus–response) reductionism?
7. Which is meant by levels of explanation?
8. Which psychological approach is linked to holism?
9. What is meant by the person-centred approach?
10. Which psychological approach is linked to reductionism?
11. Describe one way of studying the brain.
12. Does holism tell us more, or less?
13. What are the benefits of reductionism?
14. Can reductionist approaches work with human behaviour?
15. Is holism the ultimate interactionist approach?
16. Is holism the way forward with mental disorders?
17. Can you provide a modern example of the holism–reductionism debate continuing?

Glossary

Key word	Definition
Biological reductionism	An attempt to explain human behaviour with reference to the biological processes involved, e.g. genes, hormones, etc.
Conditioned reactions	Responses to stimuli that are more innate but that have been learned, particularly through the process of association.
Empathy	Being able to understand someone else's (the client's) feelings.

Key word	Definition
Endocrine system	A collection of glands that produce hormones responsible for the regulation of many functions within the human body.
Environmental (stimulus–response) reductionism	An attempt to explain human behaviour with reference to the environmental factors that impact upon it.
fMRI	Stands for Functional Magnetic Resonance Imaging and is a way of scanning the brain by showing the blood flow in different parts of the brain whilst performing certain activities.
Fully functioning person	Someone who is in touch with their deepest and innermost feelings and desires.
Genuineness	Refers to a therapist's attempt to be authentic or honest.
Gestalt	A movement in psychology that believed in the idea that 'the whole is greater than the sum of its parts'.
Gestalt laws	A set of principles created to explain the tendency to see things as a whole rather than separate elements, for example the law of closure.
Holism	The most complex explanation that tries to look at the complete picture to explain behaviour and explore all of the factors that might influence it.
Hormones	Chemicals released into the bloodstream that help to regulate many bodily functions, such as the metabolic rate.
Interactionism	An attempt to explain behaviour through the interaction of biological and environmental factors.
Levels of explanation	The different ways of explaining behaviour organised into a hierarchy of the depth of their explanation.
Multifaceted	Suggests that something has many different sides or features to it.
Neurocentrism	The tendency to focus on the brain and nervous system at the expense of other possible explanations.
Neuroimaging	The use of various techniques to either directly or indirectly image the structure and function of the nervous system.
Neurotransmitters	Chemicals that are involved in the communication through the nervous system as they are released into the synapse.
Objective	Attempting to understand something with reference only to the available evidence rather than personal opinion.
Parsimony	Refers to the idea that the simplest explanation is probably the best.

Key word	Definition
Post-mortem	Refers to something that happens after death. In this case, it refers to studying someone's brain after they have died.
Reductionism	The simplest explanation that seeks to find a single cause for behaviour.
Self-worth	How much of a favourable opinion you have of yourself.
Serotonin	A neurotransmitter that is believed to help regulate mood and social behaviour, appetite and digestion, sleep, memory, and sexual desire and function.
Synaptic transmission	The communication through the nervous system that involves electrical and chemical signals.
Unconditional positive regard	Means accepting and respecting others as they are, without judgement or evaluation.

Plenary: Exam-style questions and answers with advisory comments

Question 1.

What is meant by the holism-reductionism debate in psychology? [2 marks]

Marks for this question: AO1 = 2

Advice: In a question like this, it's important to make sure you are outlining the debate rather than just what is meant by holism and what is meant by reductionism. Although you will still need to show an understanding of the meanings of these terms to get both marks. There is no need to provide any analysis or evaluation as both of the marks are for AO1: Knowledge and understanding.

Possible answer: The debate refers to the question of to what extent we can explain behaviour with reference to one factor, e.g. biological, which provides the simplest explanation (this is reductionism). Or whether we need to refer to the full range of factors involved, e.g. biological, social, cultural, in order to provide a complete picture of behaviour (this is holism).

Question 2.

Rita and Roger are both at the same university but studying very different topics. Rita is studying physics and Roger is studying psychology. Rita is arguing that physics is better as it provides more definite explanations, whereas Roger is arguing that psychology is better as it provides more depth.

With reference to the section above, explain what is meant by levels of explanation in psychology. [3 marks]

Marks for this question: AO2 = 3

Advice: In this question, it's really important to recognise that all marks are for AO2, which means that you have to show the skill of application to the stem. You will still need to show an understanding of the levels of explanation, but this time by picking out the references from the information you have been given. There is still no need to analyse or evaluate.

Possible answer: Levels of explanation refers to the way that explanations for behaviour are organised into a hierarchy depending on their depth of explanation. Rita is arguing that physics is the best as it is more definite, tending to focus on single explanations to try to identify causes, although it would be lower down in the hierarchy as it has less depth than psychology. Roger is arguing that psychology is the best as it would be towards the top of the hierarchy as it tends to take account of more factors and therefore has more depth than physics.

Question 3.

Discuss the holism–reductionism debate in psychology. Refer to at least two topics you have studied in your answer. **[16 marks]**

Marks for this question: AO1 = 6 and AO3 = 10

Advice: This question is looking for both the skills of knowledge and understanding and those of analysis and evaluation. As there are 6 marks for AO1 and 10 for AO3, there should be greater emphasis on the evaluation. However, all such extended writing questions are marked holistically (forgive the pun) and therefore it is important that the knowledge is accurate and detailed and that the evaluation is clear and effective.

Possible answer: The holism–reductionism debate in psychology is concerned with the extent to which the behaviour of humans and animals can be explained with reference to single factors or whether we need to consider a wide range of factors in order to explain it properly.

Holism is the belief that a full understanding of behaviour can only come from a consideration of all the factors that have an influence on someone's behaviour. It is based around the Gestalt principle of 'the whole is greater than the sum of its parts' and, as such, believes that if we only focus on one part, we miss out on an understanding of how all those parts work together. For example, Rogers believed that in order to understand mental disorders, we should take a person-centred approach and an attempt to gain an understanding of what is happening in that person's life in order to understand their mental disorder.

Reductionism is the belief that the best way to explain behaviour is to look for a single cause that lies at the heart of the issue. This is based on the notion of parsimony, which believes that the simplest explanation is usually the best. An example of this in relation to mental disorders would be that if we can find a neurotransmitter imbalance that is responsible then we can alter that with drugs and provide some much needed relief for the individual.

The debate has a long history within the area of philosophy but has come to prominence in psychology due to the fact that reductionism has come to be regarded as a dirty word in the study of psychology, whereas it would be highly regarded within the more general scientific community.

The holist side is particularly associated with humanism and the work of Carl Rogers in person-centred therapy. Rogers believed that it was necessary to get a more complete and more detailed picture from the client with regard to their own problems, rather than imposing on them an explanation that lacks a full and complex understanding.

The reductionist side is particularly associated with the biological approach and the focus on factors such as genes, hormones and neurotransmitters. In recent times, the particular focus has shifted to neuroimaging techniques and the ability to isolate parts of the brain and their role in certain forms of behaviour. This has led some to brand it neurocentrism, due to its tendency to focus on these factors at the expense of any others.

The benefits of a reductionist approach are that, because it fits better with the aims of science and, in particular, the ability to predict future behaviour, it can be used to provide ways of changing problem behaviour. One example of this from environmental reductionism is the use of traffic-calming measures such as speed cameras, which has been developed from the work of Skinner into negative reinforcement. Skinner was able to get a rat to press a lever in order to prevent an electric shock by shining a yellow light just before the shock. In a similar way, speed cameras provide a big yellow box as a visual warning that you will be punished unless you press the brake lever. A simple form of stimulus–response association, but it is effective in slowing cars down, if only for a little while, till the car has past the camera.

Unfortunately, human behaviour isn't always quite so predictable as that of animals and certainly not as predictable as that of objects in the physical world. Consequently, it is not so easy to say that one person will react the same way to another just because they are exposed to the same stimulus. One example of this is in the replication of the Stanford Prison Experiment (SPE) by Reicher and Haslam in conjunction with the BBC. Using the same (although somewhat more realistic) stimulus as Phil Zimbardo, they achieved very different conclusions as the prisoners all refused to follow the rules (similar to SPE), the reaction of the guards was not to become authoritarian but to become more laissez-faire and to open up the prison cells. However, the result was similar in one way and that was when the experiment had to be cut short due to the potential for violence that had become obvious within some of the prisoners.

One of the benefits of holism is that it should provide us with a more in-depth complete explanation that should benefit us in all sorts of ways in psychology. One such area where it is beneficial is in the study of perception where Gestalt laws such as closure enable us to be able to build up a whole picture, even with incomplete information. This can be very useful for our survival as we have no need to see the whole of a predator before figuring out (possibly too late) that it is about to pounce. However, these tendencies can sometimes work against us, as we often make mistakes in perception and what we perceive to be a predator might actually just be a tree and it isn't useful to our survival for us to be afraid of trees!

Holism may be useful as a complement to other approaches though, particularly in the area of mental health. Whilst it may be useful for patients to gain temporary relief through taking drugs, it is becoming increasingly common for people to use herbal remedies and mindfulness to help with their problems in the long term. Unfortunately, as Cranford argues, much of the research into these holistic or complementary treatments is lacking in proper peer review and consequently it is difficult to check the validity of the claims made. Therefore, the effects may be no more than a placebo and whilst Cranford believes there may be a place for herbal remedies, if you want to keep the doctor away, you would be best listening to the advice of an actual doctor!

References

Cranford, N. (2014) Does holistic medicine really work? *Liberty Voice*, 23 March 2014.

Lundh, L.-G. (2015) Combining holism and interactionism. Towards a conceptual clarification. *Journal for Person-Oriented Research*, 1 (3): 185–194,

Reicher, S. and Haslam, S.A. (2006) Rethinking the psychology of tyranny: The BBC prison study. *British Journal of Social Psychology*, 45 (1): 1–40.

Rogers, C. (1951) *Client-Centered Therapy: Its Current Practice, Implications and Theory*. Boston, MA: Houghton Mifflin.

Rogers, C.R. (1961) *On Becoming a Person: A Psychotherapist's View of Psychotherapy*. Boston, MA: Houghton Mifflin.

Satel, S. and Lilienfeld, S.O. (2013) *Brainwashed: The Seductive Appeal of Mindless Neuroscience*. New York: Basic Books.

Skinner, B.F. (1965 [1953]) *Science and Human Behavior*. New York: Simon & Schuster. (Originally published by Collier Macmillan.)

Chapter 7
Idiographic and nomothetic approaches

Spec check

Idiographic and nomothetic approaches to psychological investigation.

AO1 (Knowledge and understanding): What is the basis of the debate?

One of the aims of science is to be able to predict future events based on the way that reactions have occurred in the past. One of the ways to do this is to create **general laws** that can explain how similar events will occur in the future. This debate is concerned with whether psychology should adopt that particular aim and try to create general laws or rules to be able to explain human behaviour, so that we can predict future behaviour and potentially control it or at least accommodate it in some way. This is the logic behind the **nomothetic approach**. The term nomothetic comes from the Greek word 'nomos' meaning law and this demonstrates that a nomothetic approach tries to identify laws of human behaviour that apply to all people.

On the other hand, we might consider that it's not possible to create general laws of human behaviour and instead focus purely on individuals. This would be based around the idea that human behaviour is very different from that of objects and therefore it's not possible to apply laws to it. This approach would suggest that we should recognise the uniqueness of all individuals and focus on the specific rather than the general. This is the logic behind the idiographic approach. The term idiographic comes from the Greek word 'idios' meaning private or personal and this demonstrates that an **idiographic approach** focuses on the individual nature of behaviour.

The decision to adopt one of these approaches will inevitably have an influence on the research methods that you adopt. The nomothetic approach will focus on the use of scientific methods that involve the possibility of showing cause and effect, such as experiments, and methods that allow for large numbers of people to be studied, such as surveys. The idiographic approach will focus on the use of methods that allow individuals to be studied, such as case studies, and methods that provide **qualitative** data that gives greater detail, such as unstructured interviews.

Hopefully, the difference between these two will be clear from the section above but just to make the point clearer, it might be worthwhile considering this:

When you observe some behaviour that a person shows, you could say that's just like them to do that. Or, you could say that's what always happens in this situation. The first is likely to be an idiographic description and the second might be nomothetic. Attempting to argue that phenomena always happen the same way every time is what makes something a law. That doesn't mean that you've explained why it happens, just that you're able to say that it will always happen the same way in this situation.

Just because a certain form of behaviour is demonstrated by an individual in a certain situation all the time doesn't make it a law. However, if the same behaviour is demonstrated by all people in a certain situation and it never changes, this does make it a law. At least until someone comes along and is able to show that it doesn't.

Question time

What do you think? Is it best to study behaviour generally, using lots of people in order that we can generalise to the whole population? Or, is it better to conduct individual studies in order to gain more depth and detail about human behaviour, which we can then use to gain a better understanding?

Mini plenary

One of the definitions in the list below describes an idiographic approach and one of the definitions in the list describes a nomothetic approach. Place the correct letter (select two only, from A to E) next to each of the terms above the list to indicate which definition is nomothetic and which is Idiographic.

☐ Idiographic.

☐ Nomothetic.

A An approach that focuses on the study of different cultures to ensure there is no bias.

B An approach that attempts to develop general laws/rules to explain behaviour.

C An approach that focuses on the study of the role of innate factors influencing behaviour.

D An approach that focuses on environmental influences on behaviour.

E An approach that focuses on the study of individuals to provide more detailed explanations of behaviour.

AO2 (Application of knowledge): How does the debate apply in practice?

A nomothetic approach to psychological research

Experimentation is the best way to develop scientific laws. Using experiments, you can observe aspects of behaviour and develop principles that apply to all forms of behaviour in similar circumstances. Cognitive psychology is one area of psychology that attempts to understand and predict behaviour in relation to a variety of topics. One such area is research into memory where cognitive psychologists are attempting to use experiments to show that human memory works on the basis of certain laws and that these laws can be applied in all situations.

One example of this is the **encoding specificity principle**.

Interleave me now

Encoding specificity principle

In order to understand how the principle developed, it's necessary to look at the early work of people such as Ebbinghaus (1885) who used nonsense syllables to investigate memory but who, even so, noted that the associations between items aided recall. Consequently, it was first suggested that recall was aided by **semantic associations** between words that might be generated internally and later that external factors might also play a part.

Tulving and Thomson (1973) followed a classic nomothetic approach in that they made observations based on a range of experiments conducted by other psychologists who had been working on the pre-existing **paradigm** of semantic associations, and they started to develop an idea that associations made at recall were less effective than associations made at both encoding and recall. From this they conducted their own experiments to show how the strength of the association made at encoding was important for recall, particularly when that association was also present at recall.

This was a major breakthrough as it shifted the focus of memory research away from semantic processes and towards **episodic processes**, which were to do with the events that were occurring at the time of encoding and recall, rather than the understanding of the word. The important point here is not that someone remembers the word 'chair', for example, because it is semantically related to the word 'table', but that they remember the word 'chair' because at the time of encoding it was presented in the context of the word 'table', or possibly that, at the time of encoding, they placed the word 'chair' in the context of the word 'table' (in their mind) and then later used the same cue to aid recall. A subtle difference, but an important one for our understanding of why we forget.

This new principle effectively became a new law and set the tone for future research into how memories are forgotten, as well as how they can be maintained. The logic of this led to various experiments showing how the connection between cues present at the time of encoding and recall affected retrieval and particularly that the absence of these cues caused retrieval failure. (See Table 7.1.)

Table 7.1 Research into the encoding specificity principle

Research	Finding
Goodwin et al. (1969)	An alcohol study looked at the effect of alcohol on memory and found that, when sober, items hidden when drunk couldn't be found; but they could be found when drunk again.
Godden and Baddeley (1975)	A study of divers showed that recall was 40 per cent lower when the conditions (in/out of water) at learning and recall didn't match.
Carter and Cassaday (1998)	Antihistamine drugs given at different times affected recall if taking or not taking was not matched at learning and recall.
Aggleton and Waskett (1999)	A museum study found that smells associated with Yorvik Viking museum acted as cues for recall if used at both learning and recall but didn't if not used that way.

Question time

What do these studies tell us about memory?

What does the encoding specificity principle tell us about the idiographic–nomothetic debate?

Are there any idiographic methods used in the study of memory?

Which one would be more useful?

The idiographic approach to psychological research

The research method that comes closest to our understanding of idiographic is the use of case studies. They have their origins in the field of medicine and might be better referred to there as case histories, as when a doctor looks at the medical history of a patient to gain a better understanding of the required treatment. The treatment for another patient might well be different because of the differences in the medical history of the patients, but in many ways this would combine a nomothetic approach as it would involve the use of general treatments that are not specific to the patient. Case studies have been used throughout psychological research but probably are best recognised in the work of Sigmund Freud.

Interleave me now

Sigmund Freud (1909) and the strange case of Little Hans

Freud had been contacted by a friend concerning a problem with his (soon-to-be) five-year-old son and an extreme fear of horses. The boy had seemed to become very afraid after witnessing an incident in the street in which a cart had overturned and the large horse pulling it had died. It seemed that this anxiety-provoking situation had caused the problem and the friend sought advice from Freud about what to do about it.

Freud and the friend communicated through letters, in which the boy's father would relay to Freud what the child had said and done, including what the boy had said about his dreams. One such dream was of two giraffes, one with a very long neck and the other a crumpled one. Hans recalled how he took the crumpled giraffe away from the long-necked giraffe and sat on it.

Freud interpreted this as a sign that the boy was going through the **Oedipus complex** (see Figure 7.1) and that his fear of horses was merely symbolic of his fear of castration experienced by all boys at this age.

Freud's Psychosexual Stages:	
<u>Stage/Age</u>	<u>Focus</u>
<u>Oral</u> (0–18 months)	Pleasure centers on the mouth – sucking, biting, chewing
<u>Anal</u> (18–36 months)	Pleasure focuses on bowel and bladder elimination; coping with demands for control
<u>Phallic</u> (3–6 years)	Pleasure zone is the genitals; coping with incestuous sexual feelings (*Oedipus complex*)
<u>Latency</u> (6 to puberty)	Dormant sexual feelings, identification process – gender identity
<u>Genital</u> (puberty on)	Maturation of sexual interests

Figure 7.1 Freud's psychosexual stages

Think!

What does the case of Little Hans tell us about the usefulness of an idiographic approach?

Are Freud's stages idiographic or nomothetic?

Mini plenary

Can you think of other examples of research that demonstrate the following? Place appropriate examples of research into the table under the headings of 'Idiographic approach' and 'Nomothetic approach'.

Idiographic approach	Nomothetic approach

AO3 (Analysis and evaluation of knowledge): How useful is this debate?

What are the benefits of a nomothetic approach?

The main benefit of a nomothetic approach has to be the ability to generalise to large sections of the population. If we are able to develop universal laws or rules that apply to all human beings, then we are going a long way to understanding and predicting human behaviour and mental processes. Our ability to do that opens up great possibilities for changing human behaviour for the better.

An example of this is relates to the encoding specificity principle outlined earlier. An understanding of this leads to important implications in the learning and training of anyone attempting to develop skills in a particular area. If you are trying to learn how to fly, it's probably a good idea to do it in an aeroplane, rather than a classroom and as flying takes place a long way above the ground, it might also be useful to do your training up there. If you ask any teacher what was the most useful part of their teacher training programme, it's not likely that they will say it was all the things they were taught about learning theory. Rather, they will almost certainly say that it was the time they spent in the classroom, training on the job. Similarly, when you're learning to drive, you need to do a theory test to be able to drive but that won't help you learn to drive, only being in the car on the road can do that.

This shows how important a nomothetic approach is for applying to human behaviour. If we solely take an idiographic approach, it becomes hard to apply and make practical use of. However, developing general rules for behaviour can help everyone.

What are the benefits of an idiographic approach?

The main benefit of the idiographic approach comes from the idea (mentioned earlier) of being able to use a case history to understand the needs of a particular individual. If you simply take a general approach to everything and (as suggested above) attempt to apply that rule to everyone, regardless of their individual differences, then you are likely to make mistakes and possibly, sometimes, some very important ones.

To understand this we could refer back to the example of driving and the general idea that once we are trained on the road and subjected to a general driving test that is the same for everyone, then we are OK to drive. Unfortunately, this misses out a number of important points. For example, there is no guarantee that the driving conditions will be the same for each individual and we have no idea how different individuals will cope when faced with adverse driving conditions.

As an example, Matthews and Desmond (2001) researched the effect of personality differences on a driver's response to adverse driving conditions and suggested that the response will vary depending on the personality of the driver. One example of this is that while high-anxiety individuals may respond badly to any feedback that suggests that there is a driving problem as they blame themselves for driving problems, low-anxiety individuals may respond badly to any feedback that suggests that they are invulnerable as they will behave more recklessly. This has important implications for anyone designing safety features in cars as the response to any feedback given to the driver, whilst driving, may differ depending on the individual.

It seems that in order to make valid predictions about future behaviour, it's necessary to know how different individuals will behave, rather than just how everyone will behave. This highlights the importance of having an idiographic view of behaviour.

Is an interactionist approach possible here?

This is one debate where it seems that it should be easy to adopt an interactionist approach because these two approaches inform what sort of methodological approach should be taken. Consequently, it should be easy to combine the use of methods that attempt to provide a general view, such as experiments, with those that are based on a more individual view, such as case studies. In fact, in some cases (possibly even most), it's hard to see the value in *not* adopting this approach. In methodological terms, this is referred to as **triangulation** and involves trying to make decisions based on more than one reading, or, in this case, more than one method.

One area where this combination of methods is very commonly used is in the understanding of brain function, where the general laws of brain functioning have been highlighted and, in many ways, developed from our understanding of individual cases.

For example, research into the **localisation of brain function** has often involved data from cases of individuals who were found to have some abnormality in their brain function. When Paul Broca (1861) had a man who came to be known as Tan referred to him, it gave him the opportunity to investigate the localisation of speech production in the brain. This was then used as the basis for further research into the part of the brain that is now called **Broca's area**. This has since been investigated with other individuals but, crucially, has been used as the basis for a general rule that identifies the source of speech production in the left temporal lobe.

The implications of this have been enormous for our understanding of localisation in the brain, but, more importantly, have had important effects in the application of brain surgery and the need to take greater care with certain areas of the brain. So the use of both approaches has helped both academically and practically.

Is it possible to be just nomothetic or just idiographic?

The example given earlier of an idiographic approach (Freud's case study of Little Hans) does indeed fulfil the remit of idiographic as it is based on an individual case study. However, from this and other case studies Freud went on to develop what is known in psychology as a '**grand theory**', as it is one that attempts to explain many forms of behaviour. Freud certainly developed general ideas from his case studies, so it seems that the connection between the two is much closer than we think.

However, one of the most common criticisms of Freud's work is that it lacks scientific rigour, as it is based purely upon his case studies and there is little or no experimental evidence to support his work – and therefore that it isn't possible to infer cause and effect solely from these case studies. So, maybe the use of case studies isn't so beneficial in terms of developing our understanding, as the case studies seem to place limits on that understanding rather than push it further.

Furthermore, Dronkers et al. (2007) used high resolution magnetic resonance imaging (MRI) scans to re-examine the brain of Paul Broca's most famous patient and found that the lesions in his brain extended much further than Broca's limited examination could identify, and therefore our understanding of the speech centre in the brain may be based on false data from one (or certainly just a few) case studies.

It seems as though idiographic data do have limitations, but this probably shouldn't take away from the fact that important progress was made because of the use of such data, which may be able to be refined by more controlled studies that are able to properly isolate variables further.

Is one approach more valid than the other?

The question of validity is often raised in relation to this debate, as it is frequently assumed that as nomothetic research is lab-based, **quantitative** and **objective**, then it cannot have the same level of validity as idiographic research, which is not lab-based, **qualitative** and **subjective**. However, this is far too simplistic, and it fails to take account of the different forms of validity and the subtleties that they offer.

In order to understand this issue we ought to look at different types of validity: Do they each have **internal validity**? Well, case studies may, if they provide enough detail to show what it is they were intending to, but equally lab. experiments may, as they have more tightly controlled variables that may allow them to isolate the one variable they are focused upon. Do they each have **external validity**? Well, again, case studies may, if they provide us with evidence of problems that help us to better understand other individuals with similar problems, but equally lab experiments may, if they allow us to draw out general conclusions that could be applied to large numbers of people.

The old chestnut of being lab-based and therefore lacking **ecological validity** never really works in this simplistic form, and it certainly doesn't apply in cases that are being used to further our understanding of complex human phenomenon so that we can better understand and predict future behaviour. Without lab-based research into memory, what point would there be in asking your teacher for some useful ways to revise, as they almost certainly wouldn't know.

Doesn't apply to real life? What else is it likely to apply to?

> **Think!**
>
> What do we mean by validity? Try to think of as many different types of validity as you can?
>
> Should we stop referring to ecological validity?

Mini plenary

Consider the arguments for and against an idiographic and nomothetic approach, then arrange them into two lists, as indicated below, headed Arguments for idiographic/Arguments for nomothetic. Place arguments that support both in the middle.

Arguments for idiographic	Arguments for both	Arguments for nomothetic

A modern debate: is this the end of schizophrenia?

The question of whether the diagnosis of schizophrenia is valid or not has been one that has kept psychologists busy for a long time, possibly as long as the disorder has been around. Many have questioned the whole notion of diagnosis whilst others have argued that it's not possible to refer to schizophrenia as just one disorder.

New research

The concept of schizophrenia is coming to an end – here's why

Simon McCarthy-Jones

24 August 2017

McCarthy-Jones (2017) argues that the concept of schizophrenia as a single disorder, associated with terrible hallucinations, bizarre delusions and confused thoughts, is coming to an end. The disorder seems to be going the same way as autism spectrum disorder in the suggestion that the symptoms described above actually occur along a continuum and in different degrees, with the disorder referred to as schizophrenia being at the extreme end of the spectrum. This has prompted Jim van Os, Professor of Psychiatry at Maastricht University, Netherlands, to argue that the term schizophrenia should be abolished, in favour of the term psychosis spectrum disorder.

Part of the problem with the current situation is that the life expectancy for some is reduced by two decades or more and some have been told that they would have been better off with a diagnosis of cancer as it is easier to cure. This portrayal of schizophrenia has come about, according to McCarthy-Jones, due to the view of schizophrenia as a 'hopeless, chronic brain disease' and by excluding any positive outcomes from the disorder as not having been schizophrenia at all. According to van Os, the idea of schizophrenia as a discrete brain disease is false, and the sooner we stop referring to it in this way, the better.

Further criticism has come from a top psychiatrist, Sir Robin Murray, who argues that schizophrenia as a concept is likely to come to an end soon, as we are continually able to break down the disorder into cases caused by a wide range of factors, including genetic variations, drug abuse and other social problems.

Question time

How does this article contribute to the idiographic–nomothetic debate?
Do you think we should abolish the diagnosis of schizophrenia?
What implications does this have for other mental disorders?
What is the way forward?

Chapter plenary

1. What is the basis of the idiographic–nomothetic debate?
2. What is the nomothetic approach to psychological research?
3. What is the encoding specificity principle?
4. What is the idiographic approach to psychological research?
5. What is the 'strange case of Little Hans'?
6. What are the benefits of the nomothetic approach?
7. What are the benefits of the idiographic approach?
8. Is an interactionist approach possible?
9. Is it possible to be just idiographic or just nomothetic in your approach?
10. Is one approach more valid than the other?
11. Should we stop using the term schizophrenia?

Glossary

Key word	Definition
Broca's area	The part of the brain believed to be responsible for speech production.
Ecological validity	Refers to the ability to apply the tasks employed within the research to real life.
Encoding specificity principle	States that memories are more easily retrieved if the same cues are present at both encoding and recall.
Episodic processes	Memory systems based on the time and place that the events occurred.
External validity	Refers to the ability to apply the findings of psychological research beyond the situation/participants used.
General laws	Rules of behaviour that can be applied to the whole population.
Grand theory	A psychological theory that attempts to explain all aspects of behaviour.
Idiographic approach	An approach to the study of human behaviour that is individualistic and tries to provide a more detailed understanding of single cases.
Internal validity	Refers to the measuring tools used within research being able to measure what they claim to measure.
Localisation of brain function	The idea that different parts of the brain are responsible for different forms of behaviour.
Nomothetic approach	An approach to the study of human behaviour that uses methods that allow for generalisation and the creation of general laws.
Objective	Attempting to understand something with reference only to the available evidence rather than personal opinion.
Oedipus complex	An unconscious drive experienced by boys at around the age of 3–5 that involves strong sexual feelings for their mother and hatred for their father.
Paradigm	A set way of doing or studying something that has become the established approach among most researchers.
Qualitative	Non-numerical data that is collected through methods such as observations and interviews.
Quantitative	Numerical data that is collected through such methods as experiments and surveys.
Semantic associations	Memory connections made based on the meaning of the word.

Key word	Definition
Subjective	Attempting to explain or understand something with reference to personal feelings or opinions.
Triangulation	The combination of more than one method to build up a more complete explanation.

Plenary: Exam-style questions and answers with advisory comments

Question 1.

Explain what is meant by the nomothetic approach in psychology? [2 marks]

Marks for this question: AO1 = 2

Advice: In a question like this, it's important to make sure you are clearly outlining the approach. One way of doing this is to use an example to support your explanation. There is no need to provide any analysis or evaluation as both of the marks are for AO1: Knowledge and understanding.

Possible answer: The nomothetic approach is an approach to research in psychology that focuses on the development of general laws of behaviour. An example is the analysis of experimental data by Tulving and Thomson to establish the encoding specificity principle, which shows how retrieval failure is caused by not having the same cues present at encoding and recall.

Question 2.

Explain what is meant by the idiographic approach in psychology? [2 marks]

Marks for this question: AO1 = 2

Advice: In a question like this, it's important to make sure you are clearly outlining the approach. One way of doing this is to use an example to support your explanation. There is no need to provide any analysis or evaluation as both of the marks are for AO1: Knowledge and understanding.

Possible answer: The idiographic approach is an approach to research in psychology that focuses on the study of individuals in order to provide a more in-depth understanding of behaviour. An example is the use of case studies in the work of Freud, such as that of Little Hans, from which Freud was able to further develop an understanding of the unconscious mind, which could not have been studied experimentally.

Question 3.

Researchers have found that lack of sleep in young people may be caused by exposure to technology shortly before they go to bed. A range of experiments were carried out with people between the ages of 13 and 18 years to study the effect of regular exposure to technology just before bedtime, and the results significantly showed such an effect. Some have argued that there needs to be more in-depth research with a few individuals to rule out the effects of other factors in these findings.

With reference to the section above, discuss the idiographic–nomothetic debate in psychology. [16 marks]

Marks for this question: AO1 = 6, AO2 = 4 and AO3 = 6

Advice: This question is looking for all three skills of: knowledge and understanding; application of knowledge; and analysis and evaluation. As there are 6 marks for AO1 and 6 for AO3, there should be a roughly equal emphasis on knowledge and understanding and evaluation. However, with 4 marks for AO2 in this question, there is also the need for significant reference to the material in the stem. It's important to ensure that you have shown the examiner that you have applied your knowledge to the stem, so it's always a good idea to use some of the words/sentences/phrases from the stem.

Possible answer: The idiographic–nomothetic debate in psychology is concerned with how psychologists should approach the study of human behaviour. The nomothetic side argues that we should take a scientific approach, using methods such as experiments, which allow for the isolation of variables in a controlled setting. This way we can show cause and effect and then be able to generalise this out to all human behaviour and create general laws of behaviour. This relates to the stem as it is saying that experiments were used with young people aged 13–18. The stem also refers to the experiments showing a significant effect, which suggests that a significance test was done, and they were able to produce a significant result. All of this suggests that we can predict that regular exposure to technology before bed does lead to disturbed sleep, at least in the age group studied.

The idiographic approach on the other hand would suggest that we need to carry out more detailed research, using individuals who can be researched in more detail to go beneath the surface and find out more about what else might be causing these problems. As it says in the stem, some have argued that there needs to be more in-depth research with a few individuals, which fits with the idiographic focus on case studies and other forms of qualitative research, which may provide more information. This information can help us to uncover 'the effect of other factors on these findings', so the stem is suggesting that only by probing further can we find out if there are other, more individual factors involved that are not obvious when you just look at the effect of one thing, in this case technology before bed.

The use of a nomothetic approach has allowed other general laws of behaviour to be developed, such as the encoding specificity principle in the study of memory. This principle was established by Tulving and Thomson based on their analysis of many experiments conducted by themselves and others, which continually demonstrated that having the same cues present at encoding and recall improved the chances of retrieving some previously learned information, whereas not having them led to retrieval failure. This has enormous benefits for anyone learning a new skill and has led to the use of a much more 'hands-on' approach in the development of such skills. Imagine trying to learn how to drive a car by just sitting in a classroom and having the necessary skills explained to you, or sitting an exam in a completely different environment from that which you learned the material. Crazy!

The use of an idiographic approach has allowed the development of a greater understanding of things that it is not so easy to experiment on. One example of this is the work of Sigmund Freud, who famously used case studies to develop an understanding of the influence of the unconscious mind. Freud's case study of Little Hans enabled him to develop his theory of the Oedipus complex and this led on to his 'grand theory' of the psychosexual stages, which he believed was part of the development of personality in all of us. So, from his detailed, individual case studies, Freud was able to develop a whole theory that could be applied to everyone. It seems as though the study of individual differences can enable the possibility of developing approaches that can be applied more widely.

Another example of the use of individual differences to further our understanding comes from the work of Matthews and Desmond who were able to show how personality differences affected a driver's reaction to emergency information coming from a car's control panel. They found that it wasn't quite as simple as you might imagine because both low- and high-anxiety individuals were affected in different ways, with low-anxiety individuals developing a sense of invulnerability, if they believed they were completely safe, and driving recklessly. This led to a better understanding of how to design cars to deal with these different responses.

It may be that an interactionist approach that involves the use of more than one method to triangulate the data that are available may be useful to create a complete understanding. One example of this is in the study of brain function. Paul Broca famously developed an understanding of the area of the brain believed to be localised for speech (Broca's area) through his study of a man who was known as Tan (as this was all he could say). This has allowed a general understanding of the notion of brain localisation and has been particularly important in the improved use of brain surgery by showing that surgeons need to take great care when operating on the brain as other important areas may be damaged. For example, one of the things that surgeons will do in these operations is talk to the patient to ensure that no damage is being done to their Broca's area and, in one case, they have even got a patient to play the guitar while having surgery to ensure that they did not damage anything that would affect that. This could be very important if your music is really important to you.

However, more recent examinations of the brain of Tan, by Dronkers et al., using high resolution MRI scanners, have allowed them to see that the damage to the brain extended much further than was originally thought, and this opens up the possibility of the need to change this view of the areas of the brain involved in speech as it may be that the study of this one individual was flawed.

This is a problem for case studies, as it may be that studying just one or even a few individuals in-depth not only lacks scientific rigour but also leads to flawed results that perhaps cannot and should not be applied to everyone.

References

Aggleton, J.P. and Waskett, L. (1999) The ability of odours to serve as state-dependent cues for real-world memories: Can Viking smells aid the recall of Viking experiences? *British Journal of Psychology*, 90 (1): 1–7.

Broca, P. (1861) Remarks on the seat of the faculty of articulated language, following an observation of aphemia (loss of speech). *Bulletin de la Société Anatomique*, 6: 330–357

Carter, S.J. and Cassaday, H.J. (1998) State-dependent retrieval and chlorpheniramine. *Human Psychopharmacology: Clinical and Experimental*, 13 (7): 513–523.

Dronkers, N.F., Plaisant, O., Iba-Zizen, M.T. and Cabanis, E.A. (2007) Paul Broca's historic cases: High resolution MR imaging of the brains of Leborgne and Lelong. *Brain*, 130 (5): 1432–1441.

Ebbinghaus, H. (1964) *Memory: A Contribution to Experimental Psychology* (translated by H.A. Ruger and C.E. Bussenius). New York: Dover. (Original work published in 1885.)

Freud, S. (1909) Analysis of a phobia in a five-year-old boy. *Collected papers*, Vol. III. London: Hogarth, pp. 149–295.

Godden, D.R. and Baddeley, A.D. (1975) Context-dependent memory in two natural environments: On land and underwater. *British Journal of Psychology*, 66 (3): 325–331.

Goodwin, D.W., Crane, J.B. and Guze, S.B. (1969). Alcoholic 'blackouts': a review and clinical study of 100 alcoholics. *American Journal of Psychiatry*, 126 (2): 191–198.

Matthews, G. and Desmond, P.A. (2001) Stress and driving performance: Implications for design and training. In: P.A. Hancock and P.A. Desmond (eds), *Stress, Workload and Fatigue*. Mahwah, NJ: Lawrence Erlbaum, pp. 211–231.

McCarthy-Jones, S. (2017) The concept of schizophrenia is coming to an end – here's why. *The Conversation*, 24 August 2017.

Tulving, E. and Thomson, D.M. (1973) Encoding specificity and retrieval processes in episodic memory. *Psychological Review*, 80 (5): 352–373.

Chapter 8
Ethical implications of research studies and theory

Spec check

Ethical implications of research studies and theory – including reference to social sensitivity.

AO1 (Knowledge and understanding): Ethical implications. What effect do research and theory have on those involved in research and society in general?

Ethical implications

Today, more than ever, the need for participants to be protected from the negative impact of taking part in some form of study is very clear. The impact of taking part in reality TV programmes or controversial chat shows has brought home to everyone the need for some form of consideration for the participants. As has already been seen we have ethical guidelines in order to deal with the ethical issues that arise during psychological research. **Ethical guidelines** are codes of conduct that have been developed to help psychological researchers ensure that neither the participants in the research nor the credibility of psychology are damaged during the course of research. We cannot simply absolve ourselves from the negative impact on participants, nor can we simply argue that it's all OK because at the end everyone will be debriefed and that will sort it all out. In the past, on TV programmes and in psychological studies, it has been argued that all of the participants were checked up on and were found to have suffered no long-term ill effects, and this has been used as a kind of security blanket for everyone involved to cling on to. Meanwhile, people's lives have been destroyed (or ended) while producers and researchers are consoling themselves that 'they did the right thing'. The implications of research are concerned with the wider and longer-term impact of research and theory. How does this research make people feel, even if they haven't been involved in the research itself? Do the findings and conclusions of the research impact on people's lives in some way?

Social sensitivity

The consequences of research may affect more people than simply those involved in the research process. Research can have far-reaching effects on individuals, their friends and families, and possibly even people from one particular group in society.

> **Think!**
>
> What kind of research may have consequences beyond the participants of the study? Can you think of examples of research that have affected people in society because of the way it represents their social group?

It should be clear that some research has greater potential for having a greater negative impact on certain individuals or groups in society than others. Any research that is aimed at one particular group is likely to have more of an impact, be that based on gender, ethnicity, disability, sexual orientation, religion, or any other section of society that might be easily differentiated from another. At a simple level, this could look at the driving abilities of men and women, and, at a more serious level, this could involve comparing men and women for their tendency towards child abuse! While the first of these two examples could cause problems for one gender or the other in terms of the cost of their insurance, the other could cost one gender or the other access to their children!

Socially sensitive research

The points above seem to suggest that we might be better off without conducting socially sensitive research, just as we might be better off without reality TV or controversial chat shows. However, it could be that we still have a duty to carry on with such research in spite of the ethical implications, as long as we encourage due diligence in the planning of such work. Sieber and Stanley (1988) have suggested that, whilst it is important to consider the ethics of sensitive research carefully, this should not be used as an excuse not to do it, because sensitive research deals with some of the most pressing issues facing society today.

There are four aspects of the scientific research process that raise ethical implications in socially sensitive research according to Sieber and Stanley (1988):

- **The research question**: The researcher should consider their research question carefully. Asking questions such as 'Are there racial differences in IQ?' or 'Is intelligence inherited?' may be damaging to members of a particular group.
- **The methodology used**: The researcher needs to consider the treatment of the participants and their right to *confidentiality* and *anonymity*, e.g. if a participant admits to committing a crime, should the researcher maintain confidentiality?
- **The institutional context**: The researcher should be mindful of how the data is going to be used and consider who is funding the research. If the research is

funded by a private institution or organisation, why are they funding the research and how do they intend to use the findings?

- **Interpretation and application of findings**: Finally, the researcher needs to consider how their findings might be interpreted and applied in the real world. Could their data or results be used to inform policy?

Think!

Are there certain questions that you simply shouldn't ask, or is everything open to questioning? Are some methods more socially sensitive than others, e.g. qualitative? Who should fund research? Should work that has controversial findings be banned from publication?

What if a researcher decided to study *you* to see if you were less intelligent than someone else? How would you feel? Do you think it would be OK? Maybe it would be OK to study sensitive topics if we use the following guidelines set out by Sieber and Stanley (1988):

- **Sound and valid methodology**: Often the public will often not see the flaws that academics do, e.g. Burt's intelligence tests (see Burt, 1966).
- **Justice and equitable treatment**: Research should not create prejudice or withhold treatment from a particular group. For example, Puhl and Heuer (2010) showed how stereotypes surrounding obesity led to a potential health crisis for obese people.
- **Ownership of data**: When research findings might be used to shape social policies, which affect people's lives, should they be publicly accessible? For example, Auyeung et al. (2009) at the Cambridge Autism Centre published findings showing that high levels of testosterone in amniotic fluid was a predictor of autism.
- **Cost/benefit analysis**: If the costs outweigh the potential or actual benefits, it is unethical. However, it is difficult to assess costs and benefits accurately; and the participants themselves rarely benefit from research.

Mini plenary

Using the information above and your knowledge of ethical issues and ethical guidelines, answer the following:

Ethical issues/ethical guidelines for human participants and ethical implications for socially sensitive research/suggestions for doing socially sensitive research are quite different. Identify as many similarities and differences as you can using the following table (an example is given in the table for each).

	Similarities	Differences
Ethical issues/ethical guidelines for human participants AND Ethical implications for socially sensitive research/suggestions for doing socially sensitive research.	Both are concerned with the need to avoid harm resulting from research.	Guidelines are there to protect those involved in research, whereas suggestions for socially sensitive research are there to protect all those affected even if not involved.

AO2 (Application of knowledge): How does the issue apply in practice?

Ethical implications of maternal deprivation research

Maternal deprivation is a term that has been used to describe a situation in which a child has not received adequate nurturing from their mother due to the mother being absent or neglectful. It is an area that is regarded as having ethical implications because, if you are coming up with research that is attempting to find out the effects of this, then you are almost certainly going to be looking at cases where this has happened, which may involve making judgements about someone's behaviour. While it can be easy to identify serious cases of abuse by someone, it isn't always so easy and may be more subjective to decide if someone has been neglectful. For this kind of reason, among many others, research into maternal deprivation continues to be a topic of much debate and controversy.

Interleave me now

Bowlby's **Maternal Deprivation Hypothesis** (see Bowlby, 1944) focused on the effects of early experience on later personality development and, as such, is developed as part of a psychoanalytic approach. Bowlby believed that:

> Mother love in infancy and childhood is as important for mental health as are vitamins and minerals for physical health.
>
> (Bowlby, 1953)

Bowlby believed that it was absolutely necessary for a child to receive a warm, intimate and continuous relationship with their mother or permanent mother-figure. On its own, this doesn't seem contentious, however, in his maternal deprivation hypothesis he went further and argued that if that maternal bond was broken in the early life of a child then it would lead to maternal deprivation, which in turn would result in permanent and irreversible social, intellectual and emotional problems in later life. The critical period for this was from around six months till the age of three and Bowlby argued that any break in the relationship would have consequences, and that a prolonged break could lead to the effects laid out above. And what was the role of the father to be in this situation? Essentially, simply to support the mother in doing what came naturally to her.

Undoubtedly, at the time it was made, such a declaration would make sense to many people. Europe had been going through a time of massive upheaval and the need to protect the health and welfare of children would have been paramount. However, this theory laid the foundations for what was to become a virtual doctrine in the hands of those who would argue for women to do 'what comes naturally' and stay at home and look after their children! This was based around a report commissioned by the **World Health Organization** (WHO), in line with their stated intention to deal with the large number of institutionalised children after the Second World War. Consequently, this became the dynamite that could be aimed at any woman intending to have both children and a career. Additionally, this was all happening at a time when women's liberation was about to take a massive step forward, afforded to some extent by advances in contraception and the widespread use of the contraceptive pill. These advances meant that women could now take greater control of their lives.

Question time

What are the potential implications of Bowlby's research into maternal deprivation?

Why did he do this research?

Was it reasonable to be doing this kind of research at this time?

Were there any other reasons for doing this research at this time?

Biological approach and social sensitivity

The biological approach has a number of assumptions about human behaviour, but one of the most influential is the view that behavioural characteristics are governed by genes in the same way that physical characteristics are. The basic units of heredity are called genes, which function in pairs. Behavioural geneticists study whether behavioural characteristics, such as IQ, personality, disorders, etc., are inherited in the same way as physical characteristics.

Interleave me now

The study of the **genotype** and **phenotype** allows us to understand human behaviour through an analysis of the genetic make-up of an individual and the individual differences that lie at the heart of human behaviour, which can be understood by the expression of their genotype.

Genotype is the actual genetic make-up of an individual, whereas the phenotype is the way those genes are expressed through physical, behavioural and psychological characteristics.

The Human Genome Project was set up to determine the sequence of the **human genome**, which is the complete DNA and all the genes of a human being. This was an international project aided by universities across America, Asia and Europe, including the UK, and was finished ahead of schedule in 2003. This massive accomplishment laid the ground for some great developments in medicine, biotechnology and psychology.

From the outset, those involved in the project were aware of the dangers of this research and that advances in genetics have consequences for individuals and society. Consequently, at the same time as launching the project, they also created the Ethical, Legal and Social Implications (ELSI) Program to identify and address issues raised by genomic research that would affect individuals' families and society. In particular, one of the dangers recognised was the possibility of discrimination, although at the time only discrimination in employment and insurance was mentioned. Still, it was a start.

In considering what sort of research they might have been talking about, Pilnick (2002) highlights the potential implications of finding a gene for, for example, alcoholism, aggression, intelligence or homosexuality. Pilnick suggests that such research has been linked to political movements and is particularly relevant to the eugenics movement. **Eugenics** is based around the notion that the genetic quality of humanity could be improved by the exclusion/elimination of certain genetic groups and the promotion/encouragement of other genetic groups. Essentially, the sort of thing that Hitler was in favour of.

Question time

What are the potential implications of identifying genes for the kinds of behaviours identified above (alcoholism, intelligence, homosexuality)?

Does this mean that the research shouldn't be done?

What is the point of identifying these genes?

Should we just focus on genes related to illness and disability? Are there any implications for that research?

Mini plenary

Can you think of other examples of research that do have socially sensitive implications and research that does not?

Place some examples in the table below.

Socially sensitive research	Not socially sensitive research

Now discuss those examples of research that you have identified that are not socially sensitive.

Question time

Are there really no implications arising from this research?
If no one is affected, is it really worth doing?

AO3 (Analysis and evaluation of knowledge): Is it really an issue?

What are the benefits of socially sensitive research?

Socially sensitive research can be helpful in furthering our understanding of topics that many people are ignorant about or of topics where there is a lot of stereotypical information. Examples can relate to issues of gender, race, sexuality and disability, which, once conducted, can help to reduce prejudice and discrimination against people in these groups.

The more we know, the better we are able to make informed decisions. Rather than basing our decisions on false or misguided interpretations, we might now be able to move forward with new information that can help people from certain groups to make progress.

Research into the biological basis of **transgenderism** has pointed to the existence of a sexually dimorphic nucleus in the brain, which could be responsible for a person's perception of their own gender. Consequently, people for whom their assigned gender does not fit their biological sex may simply be responding to something that is built into their DNA and not making a choice as some people suggest.

This research supports the argument made by transgender individuals that they 'have always felt like they were in the wrong body' as there is now biological evidence to suggest that is true. This may help to prevent prejudice and discrimination as **cisgender** individuals can now have greater information and understanding about the basis of this form of identity.

What are the costs of socially sensitive research?

Socially sensitive research can cause problems for certain groups if the research points the finger at them as being the cause of certain problems or possibly making something worse than it already is.

The costs of this research can create actual economic problems for both the individual and society. If the research places restrictions on the activities of certain groups, this can prevent them going about their normal business and create problems for everyone.

One example of this (although there are many) is the claimed connection between race and IQ. In their book, **The Bell Curve** (1994) (see Glossary for **bell curve**), Herrnstein and Murray claim that IQ is largely inherited with a **heritability figure** of 0.6, but, more than that, they go on to suggest that IQ is also related to ethnicity and that people from black and minority ethnic groups have a lower IQ than white people, and that this explains their poor socioeconomic position.

The implications of this are clearly bad for people from black and minority ethnic groups, as they are likely to be disregarded in the fields of employment and education if this research is believed. Furthermore, this research has been important in recent discussions in the US about the influx of Mexican immigrants into America. This might help to explain the activities of a certain American politician who, at the same time as attempting to prevent this influx, was also promoting a slogan about the need to make his country great. Is there a connection? That might just be for him to know. Nonetheless, it is having a dramatic effect on the lives of people in that position.

Is everything socially sensitive?

If we argue (as some have) that socially sensitive research involves studies that have the potential to have a negative impact on individuals from specific groups and society in general, then it could be argued that all psychological research is socially sensitive. All psychological research is ultimately about people's behaviour and, as such, will lead to some judgement or assumption about that behaviour. Even the seemingly most innocuous study could lead to some form of judgement or assumption that could negatively impact certain groups or society.

Research into **locus of control** has attempted to discover whether a person's feelings about the likely impact of their behaviour are enough to prevent people from engaging in such behaviour. This has been investigated in the realm of social change and it has been shown that those with an external locus of control, who believe that their behaviour has little impact on the end result, are less likely to engage in behaviour leading to social change – as they don't believe they have any control.

However, what if this concept is then applied to other forms of behaviour, such as a person's overall life chances, socioeconomic status or even eating behaviour? If it were found that eating disorders such as obesity were related to locus of control, could we then argue that a person's likelihood of becoming obese and developing obesity-related health problems was due to their attitudes rather than anything else, then we might be inclined to blame them more. In a situation where being obese is regarded as a choice and being anorexic is regarded as a mental health problem, this may further intensify the stereotype of obese people as 'fat and can't be bothered to do anything about it'.

Is it possible to predict the implications of research?

When conducting research, psychologists will have an interest in a particular aspect of human behaviour that they think would benefit from investigation. It's likely that they feel society would benefit from a greater understanding of the issue they have chosen to investigate. It is unlikely that they have considered all of the possible reactions that may result from this research, particularly the negative ones.

Research by Dean Hamer et al. (1993) into the genetic basis of homosexuality was able to identify a gene marker that could be responsible for some men becoming homosexual. If true, this would go against those who had argued that homosexuality is a choice that you can make in the same way that you might choose your career. Consequently, in the same way as the biological basis of transgenderism, this could be seen to have benefits for homosexual men at least. However, part of the reaction to this discovery was to suggest that homosexuality could be regarded as a genetic abnormality – leading to at least one religious leader suggesting a pre-natal test and the possibility of abortion for mothers shown to be bearing homosexual babies. Even some among the homosexual community were critical, arguing that Hamer's research might just open up another form of 'queer bashing' as homosexuality comes to be regarded as a genetic disease.

It seems unlikely that, as a homosexual man himself, Hamer had predicted this kind of reaction, and it is possible that if he had, he may have decided not to engage in such research. In fact, we know that Hamer has said that he never intended for his research to be used in this way. This suggests that it isn't always easy to predict the implications of research, even when your actual intention is to make things better.

What makes a good research question?

The decision to conduct research is a tricky one when considering the possibility that the findings could create problems of social sensitivity. This may cause researchers to hold back from conducting such research or simply create difficulties in deciding on a good topic or question to investigate.

Renzetti and Lee (1993) have suggested that there are three issues that might be considered before the creation of a good question to research:

- Is the research question looking into matters that are considered private, stressful or sacred?
- Is it likely to cause stigmatisation or fear?

- Is there a political threat in areas of research that may cause controversy or social conflict.

Unfortunately, this may mean that most research questions become socially sensitive and therefore there may be no such thing as a good research question. McCosker et al. (2001) argues that further problems arise as the sensitivity of the research may not be apparent at the start of the research but, equally, a subject that was believed to be socially sensitive at the start may turn out no to be. She gives the example of research into abuse against women in which the women interviewed report feeling relieved that they were given the chance to talk about their experiences.

This shows that it may be extremely difficult to come up with a good research question, although as McCosker demonstrates, just because it may appear to be socially sensitive doesn't mean that someone should not carry it out.

Mini plenary

Consider the arguments made above, both for and against the decision to carry out socially sensitive research. What do you think? Use a separate piece of paper to create a plan of the arguments for and against and then, in no more than 100 words, explain whether you think we should conduct socially sensitive research or not in the space below.

Plan:
Arguments for:
Arguments against:

Your response:

A modern issue: religious fundamentalism

Whilst **religious fundamentalism** isn't exactly a new phenomenon and has probably existed in some form since the first religious ideas came to be, it is something that continues to engage and encourage debate in modern times. It is often taken for granted that fundamentalists have been brainwashed in some way and that is why they have become the way they are. New research suggests that their brains may not just be washed but actually damaged.

New research

Are religious fundamentalists brain-damaged?

John Stonestreet and Roberto Rivera

Christian Post, 5 February 2019

In this article, the question of recent attempts to explain religious fundamentalism is compared to children's stories originally published in 1902 by Rudyard Kipling that became known as the 'Just So Stories'. The stories were made-up explanations for how animals developed certain characteristics, told in the same way each time to Kipling's daughter because she demanded them to be told 'just so'. The term was more recently used In 1976, by the palaeontologist Stephen Jay Gould, as a way of expressing his feelings about the developing field of evolutionary psychology and has since come to refer to anything that involves an unsubstantiated claim for some form of animal or human behaviour.

Stonestreet and Rivera suggest that the most recent 'just so story' comes from the suggestion that there is a link between religious fundamentalism and brain damage. They refer to a study, 'Biological and Cognitive Underpinnings of Religious Fundamentalism' (Zhong et al., 2017), published in the journal *Neuropsychologia*, in which the data from more than a hundred Vietnam war veterans had been examined specifically because it was known that a large number of them had damage to an area of the brain that is apparently believed to play a role in fundamental religious beliefs.

Stonestreet and Rivera suggest that this procedure stinks of **confirmation bias**, as the researchers specifically set out to find evidence to confirm their belief. Rather than choosing one hundred random people to examine, they chose more than a hundred who were known to have this form of damage. Using this sample compared to a control group of non-damaged veterans, the researchers were able to identify damage to an area of the prefrontal cortex from CT scans with both groups.

Stonestreet and Rivera question the definition of religious fundamentalism used by the researchers, which was 'an ideology that emphasises traditional religious texts and rituals and discourages progressive thinking about religion and social issues', as they argue that this describes pretty much every **Abrahamic religion**, not just the fundamentalist version. This definition was then applied to the findings of the CT scans as the researchers suggested that damage to that area of the brain causes 'a reduction in cognitive flexibility and openness', which leads to 'an increase in religious fundamentalism'.

The article goes further to question whether the researchers could be certain that the veterans were actually religious fundamentalists or had just answered questions on a questionnaire that led the researchers to assume that they were religious fundamentalists. Furthermore, the article questions the researchers own 'cognitive flexibility and openness' as they seem to have a very narrow view of religious belief, leading the authors to question whether the researchers might be brain-damaged fundamentalists too – even going so far as to suggest that the description of religious fundamentalists used might just as easily be applied to a number of then-current US presidential candidates giving rise to the question of whether they are also brain-damaged!

Question time

What are the ethical implications of this research?

Which groups of people are affected by this? Is it likely to be just religious fundamentalists?

Why do you think they refer to this as a form of confirmation bias?

What is the way forward? Is there any way we can deal with this issue?

Chapter plenary

1. What is meant by the term ethical implications?
2. What is meant by the term social sensitivity?
3. What are the four aspects of the research process that raise ethical implications in socially sensitive research according to Sieber and Stanley (1988)?
4. What are the additional guidelines for studying sensitive topics?
5. What are the similarities and differences between ethical issues/guidelines for human participants and the ethical implications/additional guidelines for socially sensitive research?
6. What are the potential ethical implications of Bowlby's maternal deprivation research?
7. What are the potential ethical implications of the study of the genotype and phenotype?
8. Do these implications mean that research shouldn't be done in these areas?

9. What other examples of research in psychology are there that are relevant to this issue?
10. What are the benefits of socially sensitive research?
11. What are the costs of socially sensitive research?
12. Is everything socially sensitive?
13. Is it possible to predict the implications of research?
14. What makes a good research question?
15. Can you provide modern examples of socially sensitive research?

Glossary

Key word	Definition
Abrahamic religion	Religious organisations that believe that the prophet Abraham and his descendants have a particularly important role in spiritual development, e.g. Judaism, Christianity and Islam.
Anorexic	Having an abnormally low body weight that may put someone at risk of serious illness or death.
Bell curve	Refers to a normally distributed population in which the distribution of a set of data creates a single curve that resembles the shape of a bell. IQ is believed to be normally distributed with a few people at either end of the scale.
Cisgender	Having a gender identity or expression that matches your assigned sex.
Confirmation bias	The tendency to only focus on phenomena that agree with your pre-existing view and ignore any that disagree.
Equitable	The process of making something equal for everyone.
Ethical guidelines	Suggestions for how to conduct psychological research fairly and in a way that allows participants to leave in the same state that they came into the research.
Ethical implications	The possible impact of psychological research on individuals or groups in society.
Eugenics	A set of beliefs that it is possible to improve the genetic quality of the population by excluding certain genetic groups.
Genotype	The genetic make-up of an individual.
Heritability figure	Refers to the proportion of a characteristic that is due to either genetics or environmental influence. A high heritability figure suggests that the proportion influenced by genes is higher than the proportion influenced by the environment.

Key word	Definition
Human genome	The complete set of genes contained within a human organism.
Locus of control	The idea that control over your life chances is either 'located' within you (you have control) or elsewhere (others have control).
Methodology	The methods of research that are employed when studying a particular psychological phenomenon.
Obesity	Having a body mass index that is higher than 30.
Phenotype	The observable characteristics of an individual resulting from the interaction of their genotype with the environment.
Religious fundamentalist	Someone who follows the teachings of a religion to the letter with no interpretation and believes in the absolute authority of those teachings and/or of God(s).
Sacred	Something that has religious significance and is very highly regarded by a religious group or orthodoxy.
Social sensitivity	The recognition that psychological research can affect more than just the individuals involved in the research – it can also affect other individuals and groups in society.
Stigmatisation	Describing or regarding someone/something as worthy of disapproval.
Transgenderism	The belief in the possibility of having a gender identity or expression that differs from your assigned sex.
World Health Organization	The group created to monitor the health of the whole population of the planet.

Plenary: Exam-style questions and answers with advisory comments

Question 1.

Explain what is meant by socially sensitive research in psychology?

[2 marks]

Marks for this question: AO1 = 2

Advice: In a question like this, it's important to make sure you are making it clear what type of research is involved, so this will probably require an example. There is no need to provide any analysis or evaluation as both marks are for AO1: Knowledge and understanding.

Possible answer: This refers to any research that has ethical implications for society or certain groups in society. An example of this could be research into maternal deprivation, which implies that women are 'bad mothers' for leaving their children in care while they go to work.

Question 2.

In 2003, an accurate and complete human genome sequence was finished and made available to scientists and researchers. The finished sequence covers 99 per cent of the human genome's gene-containing regions to an accuracy of 99.9 per cent. The project was able to map 3.7 million SNPs or genetic variations that may be responsible for diseases or traits.

Discuss the ethical implications of socially sensitive research in psychology with reference to the section above. [16 marks]

Marks for this question: AO1 = 6, AO2 = 4 and AO3 = 6

Advice: This question is looking for all three skills of: knowledge and understanding; application of knowledge; and analysis and evaluation. As there are 6 marks for AO1 and 6 for AO3, there should be a roughly equal emphasis on knowledge and understanding and evaluation. However, with 4 marks for AO2 on this question, there is also the need for significant reference to the material in the stem. It's important to ensure that you have shown the examiner that you have applied your knowledge to the stem, so it's always a good idea to use some of the words/sentences/phrases from the stem.

Possible answer: Socially sensitive research refers to any research that may have ethical implications for society or for particular groups within that society. The sorts of implications that might occur are that certain groups may be regarded more negatively than others and, as such, be subject to prejudice or discrimination. This creates problems for psychological researchers as they will need to consider a number of aspects of the research process before proceeding and Sieber and Stanley have identified four such aspects. The research question itself should be considered, as some questions could be damaging, e.g. is there a connection between race and IQ? The researchers should also consider the methodology used as they may infringe upon people's rights, e.g. to maintain confidentiality. In addition, the institution that is funding the research should be considered, as some institutions may have a vested interest in certain findings, e.g. oil companies looking into the effect of global warming. And finally the interpretation and application of the findings need to be considered, as the findings might be used in a way that wasn't originally intended, e.g. the item above refers to research by the human genome project and their 'completion of the human genome sequence'.

One of the issues connected with studying the effect of genes upon human traits is that it could lead to the idea that some groups in society are naturally inferior to others. If you discover that IQ is genetic then you could argue that some people/groups are genetically less intelligent, which has implications for the way such people are treated in society. For example, Cyril Burt's research appeared to show a strong level of heritability in intelligence and Burt was given a role as an educational adviser in the government. Unfortunately, it was later revealed that Burt's work wasn't conducted in the way he suggested, which brought his results into question.

Sieber and Stanley have gone further with this and suggested that there should be further ethical guidelines to help deal with such matters. They suggest that research should be assessed to ensure that it has sound and valid methods, that it will lead to equitable treatment for all those affected, that consideration should be given to whether the findings should be publicly accessible and that the costs and benefits should be considered beforehand.

In relation to the item above, there are potential issues here as, although we can be sure that the human genome project used sound and valid methodology, we would still have to question whether all their findings should be publicly accessible, although there would equally be ethical questions asked about holding such information back.

One problem that arose from making research public came from the research of Dean Hamer into homosexuality. He found that, once it was announced that his research claimed to have discovered a gene for homosexuality in men, there was an outcry suggesting that it may now be possible to provide a prenatal test for homosexuality with the possibility of abortion being offered to those affected. As a gay man himself, it's unlikely that Hamer had foreseen this outcome and it shows that it may be difficult to foresee the implications of such research.

This highlights the issue of identifying 'SNPs or genetic variations in human diseases or traits'. If we accept that, when we identify genetic variations that lead to disease, we can attempt to intervene in some way to change that, then we need to address the question of whether we should do the same with human traits, e.g. aggression. In fact, such trait variations may come to be regarded as diseases, simply because they are investigated in the same way.

Pilnick has suggested that one of the dangers of doing research into the genes associated with aggression or alcoholism, or indeed homosexuality, is that it is often linked with the idea of eugenics and the belief that it is possible to eliminate certain traits in order to create a more genetically pure human population that isn't troubled by such issues. Unfortunately, there is a short step from this to the sort of activities undertaken by Hitler to create a human master race under the Nazis.

There are clearly many potential costs associated with such research, but there may also be some benefits. Although it may be problematic attempting to come up with a research question that is acceptable in the minefield of social sensitivity, it is also worth saying that, just because something is socially sensitive, it doesn't mean it shouldn't be studied. As McCosker argues, a question that is believed to be socially sensitive at the start may turn out not to be. She uses the example of abuse against women in which the victims were relieved to be able to talk about their experiences – something that they may not have had the chance to do if the research had not been conducted.

Another example of this is research into transgenderism, which may appear to be highly socially sensitive as there is a clearly identifiable group that could be affected. However, research has found that there may be a sexually dimorphic nucleus in the brain that is responsible for the differences between cisgender and transgender people. This finding challenges the misconception that transgenderism is a choice rather than a biological fact. Similar to the findings of the human genome project, it may be that transgenderism is built into the DNA of some people and this could, hopefully, provide a better understanding of why some people are transgender, which could actually improve society's treatment of that group of people, rather than make it worse.

References

Auyeung, B., Baron-Cohen, S., Ashwin, E., Knickmeyer, R., Taylor, K. and Hackett, G. (2009) Fetal testosterone and autistic traits. *British Journal of Psychology*, 100 (1): 1–22.

Bowlby, J. (1944) Forty-four juvenile thieves: Their characters and home-life. *International Journal of Psychoanalysis*, 25: 19–53 and 107–128.

Bowlby, J. (1953) *Child care and the Growth of Love*. London: Penguin Books.

Burt, C. (1966) The genetic determination of differences in intelligence: A study of monozygotic twins reared together and apart. *British Journal of Psychology*, 57 (1–2): 137–153.

Hamer, D.H., Hu, S., Magnuson, V.L., Hu, N. and Pattatucci, A.M. (1993) A linkage between DNA markers on the X chromosome and male sexual orientation. *Science*, 261 (5119): 321–327.

Herrnstein, R.J. and Murray, C. (1994) *The Bell Curve: Intelligence and Class Structure in American Life*. New York. Free Press.

McCosker, H., Barnard, A. and Gerber, R. (2001). Undertaking sensitive research: Issues and strategies for meeting the safety needs of all participants. In *Forum Qualitative Sozialforschung (Forum: Qualitative Social Research)*, 2 (1).

Pilnick, A. (2002) What 'most people' do: Exploring the ethical implications of genetic counselling. *New Genetics and Society*, 21 (3): 339–350.

Puhl, R.M. and Heuer, C.A. (2010) Obesity stigma: Important considerations for public health. *American Journal of Public Health*, 100 (6): 1019–1028.

Renzetti, C.M. and Lee, R.M. (1993) *Researching Sensitive Topics*. Newbury Park, CA: Sage.

Sieber, J.E. and Stanley, B. (1988) Ethical and professional dimensions of socially sensitive research. *American Psychologist*, 43 (1): 49.

Stonestreet, J. and Rivera, R. (2019) Are religious fundamentalists brain-damaged? *Christian Post: Voices*, 5 February 2019. www.christianpost.com/voice.

Zhong, W., Cristofori, I., Bulbulia, J., Krueger, F. and Grafman, J. (2017) Biological and cognitive underpinnings of religious fundamentalism. *Neuropsychologia*, 100: 18–25.

Index

#metoo 17, 22

Abrahamic religion 123, 124
abuse against women 121
adoption studies 69–70
anorexic 120, 124
attachment: cultural bias 29–31; strange situation 29–30; type 26, 29–31, 39–40; Van Ijzendoorn and Kroonenberg 30–31, 32, 39–40; parenting style 32, 39–40; intercultural and intracultural differences 32; construct equivalence 32, 39–40; Ainsworth 29–30, 39–40; Western research methods 32
authoritarian personality 27

Bandura, A. 43, 57–59
bell curve 119, 124
bias 8–9, 24–25
biological approach 116
biological reductionism 81, 91
black lives matter 35
Blass, T. 28
Bowlby, J.: attachment theory 11; monotropy 11; primary attachment figure 11; maternal deprivation hypothesis 115–116; critical period 116
brain localisation 103, 107, 110
brain scanning: CAT 84; fMRI 85, 92; neuroimaging 85, 92; neurocentrism 85, 92, 95
Broca's area 103, 107, 110
Buss, D. 33–34, 40

case studies 100, 111
cause and effect 72, 78, 88
cisgender 73–74, 75, 119, 124, 127
conditioned reactions 82, 91
confirmation bias 122, 124
cost-benefit analysis 114, 118–119, 124, 127
cultural bias: ethnocentrism 25, 39–40; imposed etic 26, 33–34, 39–40
cultural relativism 25–26, 32–33, 39–40
cultural stereotypes 34–36

depression statistics 12
determinism: concept of 42, 45, 57–59; hard 43, 45, 57–59; soft 43, 45, 50–51, 57–59; biological 43, 45, 57–59; environmental 43, 45, 57–59; psychic 43–44, 45, 57–59; readiness potential 50–51, 57–59; cognitive neuroscience 51, 57–59; and criminal responsibility 52–54, 57–59
diathesis-stress model 70–71, 78

Ebbinghaus, H. 99
Ellis's ABC model 12;
emic approach 26, 33–34, 39–40
empathy 84, 91,
encoding specificity principle 99–100, 102, 107, 108, 109
endocrine system 81, 92
environmental influence: concept of 61, 63, 68, 75, 77; and changing behaviour 69–70
environmental reductionism 80–81, 87, 92, 95
epigenetics 71, 78
epigenome 71, 75
episodic processes 99, 107
ethical guidelines 112, 114–115, 124
ethical implications 112, 114–115, 124
eugenics 117, 124, 127
external validity 104, 107

feminist research 15, 22
free will: concept of 42; and Humanistic psychology 45, 57–59; benefits 49; possibility of 50,
Freud: psychodynamic approach 10–11; psychosexual development 9–10, 101; psychic determinism 43–44; case studies 101, 108, 110; Little Hans 101, 108, 110; Oedipus complex 101, 107, 110
functionally universal 33, 40

gender bias: Androcentrism 9, 21–22; Alpha bias 9, 21–22; Beta bias 10, 21–22

general laws 97, 102, 107, 109
genetics: influence of 61, 63, 68; and future
    behaviour 68–69; and vulnerability 71,
    78; and homosexuality 120; variations
    126–127
genotype 62, 71, 75, 78, 117, 124
genuineness 84, 92
Gestalt psychology 80, 86, 92, 94
grand theory 104, 107
gynocentric 22

Hamer, D. 120, 127
heritability figure 119, 124
holistic medicine 89, 95–96
homosexuality 120, 127
hormones 81, 92, 95
human genome 117, 125, 126–128
Humanist Approach 83–84

idiographic approach: benefits of 102–103;
    concept of 97–98; validity of 104;
    arguments for 105
implicit biases: gender 9; racism 35–36
institutional bias 14
interactionist approach 62, 78, 88, 92, 103,
    110
internal validity 104, 107
IQ 119, 126

Kohlberg 10

levels of explanation 82, 92, 94
locus of control 119–120, 125

Maslow: hierarchy of needs 45; self-
    actualisation 45, 57–59; benefits of free
    will 49–50,
maternal deprivation 115, 126
Mead, M. 33–34, 40
mental health and culture 34, 40,
methodological validity 114
Milgram, S. 27–28

nature: and the biological approach 63;
    and innate characteristics 60–61, 63,
    75; pre-programmed behaviour 60,
    76, 77; inherited behaviour 61,
    75
neuroticism and gender 14, 21–22
neurotransmitters 64, 76, 81, 92
nomothetic approach: benefits of 102;
    concept of 97–98; validity of 104;
    arguments for 105

nurture: and learned behaviour 61, 63, 75;
    and influence of upbringing 61, 76: and
    the behavioural approach 66, classical
    conditioning 66–68, 75

obesity 119–120, 125
objective 83, 87, 92, 104, 107

paradigm 99, 107
parenting style 32
parsimony 81, 92, 94
person-centred approach 84, 89, 94–95
phenotype 62, 71, 76, 117, 125
phobias 67–68
psychosis spectrum disorder 105–106

qualitative 104, 107, 109
qualitative methods 83, 97
quantitative 104, 107, 109

racial profiling 35
religious fundamentalism 122–123, 125
Rogers, C. 83–84, 94–95

science and sexism 14
schizophrenia 105–106
schizophrenogenic mother 5–6
scientific emphasis on causal explanations:
    general laws 44; limitations 51; positivist
    approach 51–52; qualitative approach
    51–52,
self-worth 84, 89, 93
semantic associations 99, 107
serotonin 88, 93
sexual discrimination legislation 15–16
sexual misconduct 17
sexually dimorphic nucleus 118, 127
Sieber and Stanley 113–114, 126–127
Skinner, B.F.: Behavioural approach 47;
    environmental determinism 43, 57–59;
    schedules of reinforcement 47–48;
    negative reinforcement 87, 95
Smith and Bond 24, 39
SNPs 126–127
social influence and culture bias 27–28
social sensitivity 113, 116, 125–127
socialisation and gender 14
socially sensitive research 113–115, 118,
    119, 121, 125–127
stigmatisation 120, 125
subjective 104, 108
synaptic transmission: concept of 81, 93;
    and action potential 64, 65,

the implications of: alpha bias 14; beta bias 15; ethnocentrism 34
transgender 73–74, 76
transgenderism 118, 120, 125, 127–128
triangulation 103, 108, 110
Tulving and Thompson 99

unconditional positive regard 84, 93
uniqueness 97
universality 8–9, 24–25, 32–34

value freedom 9

Watson, J.: Little Albert 67
Weinstein moment 17
World Health Organisation 116, 125

Zimbardo, P. 87, 95
Zuckerman and sensation seeking 65–66

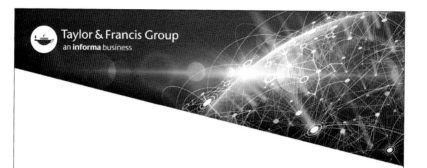